RUSSIA
THE INGUSH-OSSETIAN CONFLICT IN THE PRIGORODNYI REGION

Human Rights Watch/Helsinki

Human Rights Watch
New York • Washington • London • Brussels

Copyright © May 1996 by Human Rights Watch.
All rights reserved.
Printed in the United States of America.

Library of Congress Catalogue Number: 96-75960
ISBN: 1-56432-165-7

Human Rights Watch/Helsinki
Human Rights Watch/Helsinki was established in 1978 to monitor and promote domestic and international compliance with the human rights provisions of the 1975 Helsinki Accords. It is affiliated with the International Helsinki Federation for Human Rights, which is based in Vienna, Austria. Holly Cartner is the executive director; Erika Dailey, Rachel Denber, Christopher Panico and Diane Paul are research associates; Ivan Lupis is the research assistant; Anne Kuper, Alexander Petrov, and Shira Robinson are associates. Jonathan Fanton is the chair of the advisory committee and Alice Henkin is vice chair.

HUMAN RIGHTS WATCH

Human Rights Watch conducts regular, systematic investigations of human rights abuses in some seventy countries around the world. It addresses the human rights practices of governments of all political stripes, of all geopolitical alignments, and of all ethnic and religious persuasions. In internal wars it documents violations by both governments and rebel groups. Human Rights Watch defends freedom of thought and expression, due process and equal protection of the law; it documents and denounces murders, disappearances, torture, arbitrary imprisonment, exile, censorship and other abuses of internationally recognized human rights.

Human Rights Watch began in 1978 with the founding of its Helsinki division. Today, it includes five divisions covering Africa, the Americas, Asia, the Middle East, as well as the signatories of the Helsinki accords. It also includes five collaborative projects on arms transfers, children's rights, free expression, prison conditions, and women's rights. It maintains offices in New York, Washington, Los Angeles, London, Brussels, Moscow, Dushanbe, Rio de Janeiro, and Hong Kong. Human Rights Watch is an independent, nongovernmental organization, supported by contributions from private individuals and foundations worldwide. It accepts no government funds, directly or indirectly.

The staff includes Kenneth Roth, executive director; Cynthia Brown, program director; Holly J. Burkhalter, advocacy director; Barbara Guglielmo, finance and administration director; Robert Kimzey, publications director; Jeri Laber, special advisor; Gara LaMarche, associate director; Lotte Leicht, Brussels office director; Juan Méndez, general counsel; Susan Osnos, communications director; Jemera Rone, counsel; and Joanna Weschler, United Nations representative.

The regional directors of Human Rights Watch are Peter Takirambudde, Africa; José Miguel Vivanco, Americas; Sidney Jones, Asia; Holly Cartner, Helsinki; and Christopher E. George, Middle East. The project directors are Joost R. Hiltermann, Arms Project; Lois Whitman, Children's Rights Project; Gara LaMarche, Free Expression Project; and Dorothy Q. Thomas, Women's Rights Project.

The members of the board of directors are Robert L. Bernstein, chair; Adrian W. DeWind, vice chair; Roland Algrant, Lisa Anderson, Alice L. Brown, William Carmichael, Dorothy Cullman, Irene Diamond, Edith Everett, Jonathan Fanton, James C. Goodale, Jack Greenberg, Alice H. Henkin, Stephen L. Kass, Marina Pinto Kaufman, Harold Hongju Koh, Alexander MacGregor, Josh Mailman, Andrew Nathan, Jane Olson, Peter Osnos, Kathleen Peratis, Bruce Rabb, Orville Schell, Sid Sheinberg, Gary G. Sick, Malcolm Smith, Nahid Toubia, Maureen White, and Rosalind C. Whitehead.

Addresses for Human Rights Watch
485 Fifth Avenue, New York, NY 10017-6104
Tel: (212) 972-8400, Fax: (212) 972-0905, E-mail: hrwnyc@hrw.org

1522 K Street, N.W., #910, Washington, DC 20005-1202
Tel: (202) 371-6592, Fax: (202) 371-0124, E-mail: hrwdc@hrw.org

33 Islington High Street, N1 9LH London, UK
Tel: (171) 713-1995, Fax: (171) 713-1800, E-mail: hrwatchuk@gn.apc.org

15 Rue Van Campenhout, 1000 Brussels, Belgium
Tel: (2) 732-2009, Fax: (2) 732-0471, E-mail: hrwatcheu@gn.apc.org

Gopher Address://gopher.humanrights.org:port5000
Listserv address: To subscribe to the list, send an e-mail message to majordomo@igc.apc.org with "subscribe hrw-news" in the body of the message (leave the subject line blank).

ACKNOWLEDGMENTS

This report is based on a trip to the Republic of Ingushetiya, hereafter Ingushetiya, and the Republic of North Ossetia-Alaniya, hereafter North Ossetia, both states of the Russian Federation, from August 11-19, 1994. Until 1994, North Ossetia was the North Ossetian Autonomous Soviet Socialist Republic (ASSR), a part of the former Soviet Union. Until 1992, Ingushetiya was part of the Checheno-Ingush Autonomous Soviet Socialist Republic (ASSR), and was also part of the former Soviet Union. Human Rights/Helsinki representatives visited Vladikavkaz, Kartsa, Chermen, Tarskoye, Kurtat, Dachnoye, and Maiskii in North Ossetia and Nazran and Gaziyurt in Ingushetiya. Jeri Laber and Rachel Denber edited the report, and Shira Robinson provided production assistance for its publication.

Human Rights Watch/Helsinki thanks both North Ossetian and Ingush authorities as well as officials from the Russian Temporary Administration (now the Temporary State Committee) for their cooperation with the mission participants. Human Rights Watch/Helsinki would like to express our appreciation to all those who read the report and commented on it, including Prof. John Collarusso of McMaster University. We would also like to thank the members of the Russian human rights group *Memorial*, who provided generous assistance and advice. In 1994 *Memorial* published an excellent report on the conflict in the Prigorodnyi region, *"Two Years after the War: The Problem of the Forcibly Displaced in the Area of the Ossetian-Ingush Conflict."* Finally, we would like to thank the Carnegie Corporation of New York, the Henry Jackson Fund, the Merck Fund and the Moriah Fund for their support.

Human Rights Watch/Helsinki takes no position on the ultimate status of the Prigorodnyi region. Our sole concern is conformance with international humanitarian law.

CONTENTS

I. SUMMARY AND RECOMMENDATIONS 1
    BACKGROUND 2
    RECOMMENDATIONS 4

II. DEMOGRAPHY AND ETHNOGRAPHY 6

III. BACKGROUND TO THE CONFLICT 9
    DEPORTATIONS UNDER STALIN 9
    INGUSH RETURN TO THE PRIGORODNYI REGION 10
    NATIONAL TENSIONS INCREASE UNDER PERESTROIKA 15
    LAW ON THE REHABILITATION OF REPRESSED PEOPLES 18
    BREAKAWAY OF CHECHNYA AND THE CREATION OF
        THE REPUBLIC OF INGUSHETIYA 22
    THE ROLE OF SOUTH OSSETIANS IN THE CONFLICT 24
    THE ARMING OF OSSETIANS AND INGUSH 29

IV. 1992: TENSIONS AT A BOIL 31
    CHRONOLOGY OF THE EVENTS IMMEDIATELY
        PRECEDING THE ARMED CONFLICT 33

VI. 1992-1994: VIOLATIONS OF THE RULES OF WAR
        IN THE INGUSH-OSSETIAN CONFLICT 36
    DACHNOYE 38
        Violations by Ossetian Forces 38
    CHERMEN 38
        Violations by Ingush Forces 39
        Violations by Ossetian Forces 44
    KARTSA 45
        Violations by Ossetian Forces 45
        Violations by Ingush Forces 51
    KURTAT 51
        Violations by Ossetian Forces 51
        Violations by Ingush Forces 53
    VLADIKAVKAZ 55
        Violations by Ossetian Forces 55
    ZAVODSKII (A SUBURB OF VLADIKAVKAZ) 56
        Violations by Ossetians Forces 56
    TARSKOYE 57
        Violations By Ossetian Forces 57
    OTHER VIOLATIONS IN 1994 59
    OFFICIAL RUSSIAN CASUALTY FIGURES 60

VI. RUSSIAN POLICY AND CONDUCT 62
    THE TEMPORARY ADMINISTRATION 62
    CULPABILITY OF THE RUSSIAN GOVERNMENT 64

VII. CONCLUSION OF THE CONFLICT 73
    ACCOUNTABILITY AND JUSTICE IN
        THE PRIGORODNYI CONFLICT 73
    RECONCILIATION AND THE RETURN OF THE DISPLACED 79
        Negotiations and Decrees 79
        Number of Repatriated Ingush 80
        Obstacles to Return 82

VIII. RECENT DEVELOPMENTS 90

IX. VIOLATIONS OF INTERNATIONAL HUMANITARIAN
        AND HUMAN RIGHTS LAW 95
    PROHIBITION OF ATTACKS AGAINST CIVILIANS 96
    PROHIBITION OF INDISCRIMINATE ATTACKS:
        THE RULE OF PROPORTIONALITY 97
    OTHER PROHIBITED ACTS 97
        Violence to Life and Person 98
        Hostage-Taking 98
        Humiliating or Degrading Treatment 98
        Looting or Pillage 98
        Displacement of Civilians and Attacks on Civilian Objects 99
    VIOLATIONS OF INTERNATIONALLY-RECOGNIZED
        HUMAN RIGHTS 100

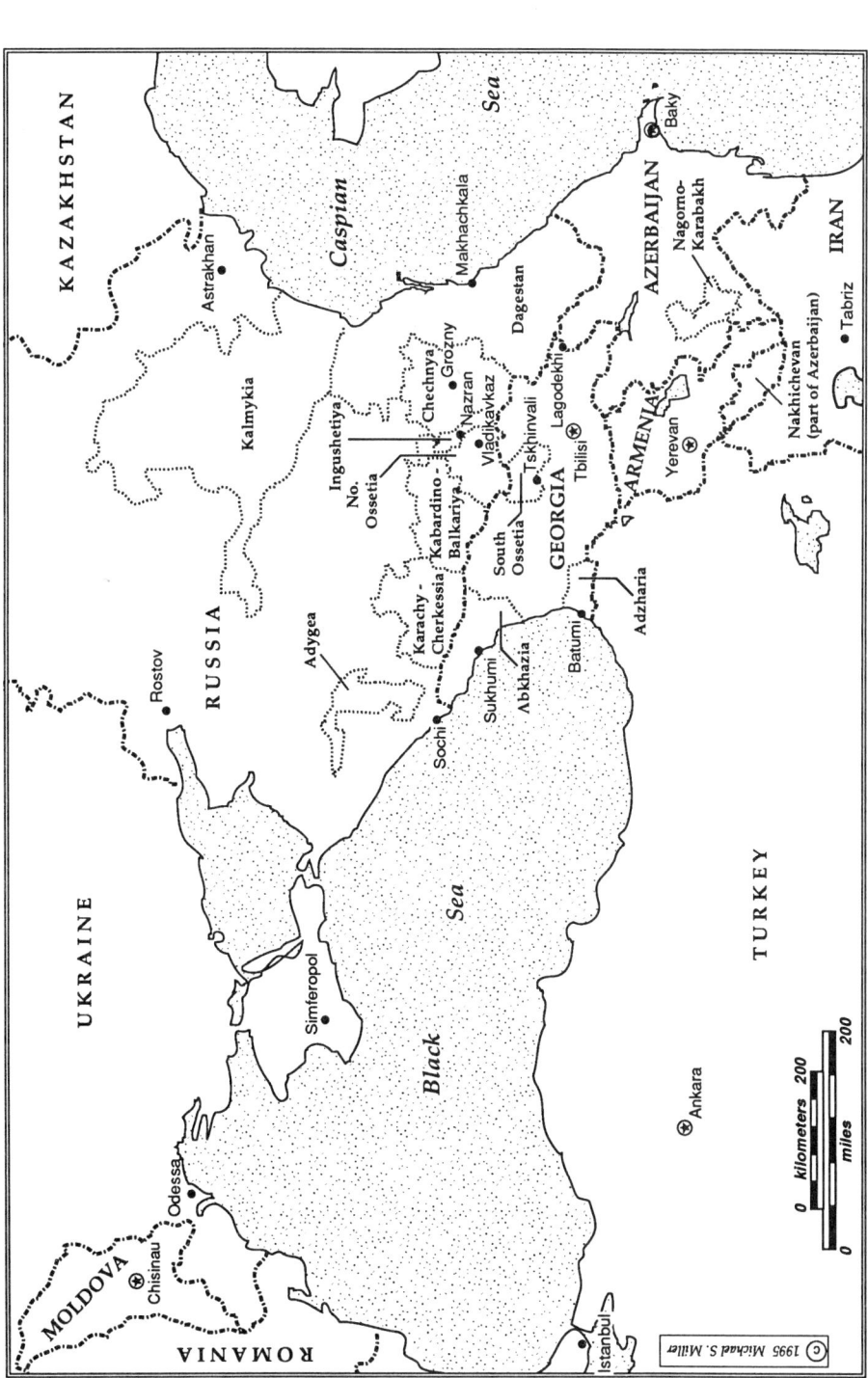

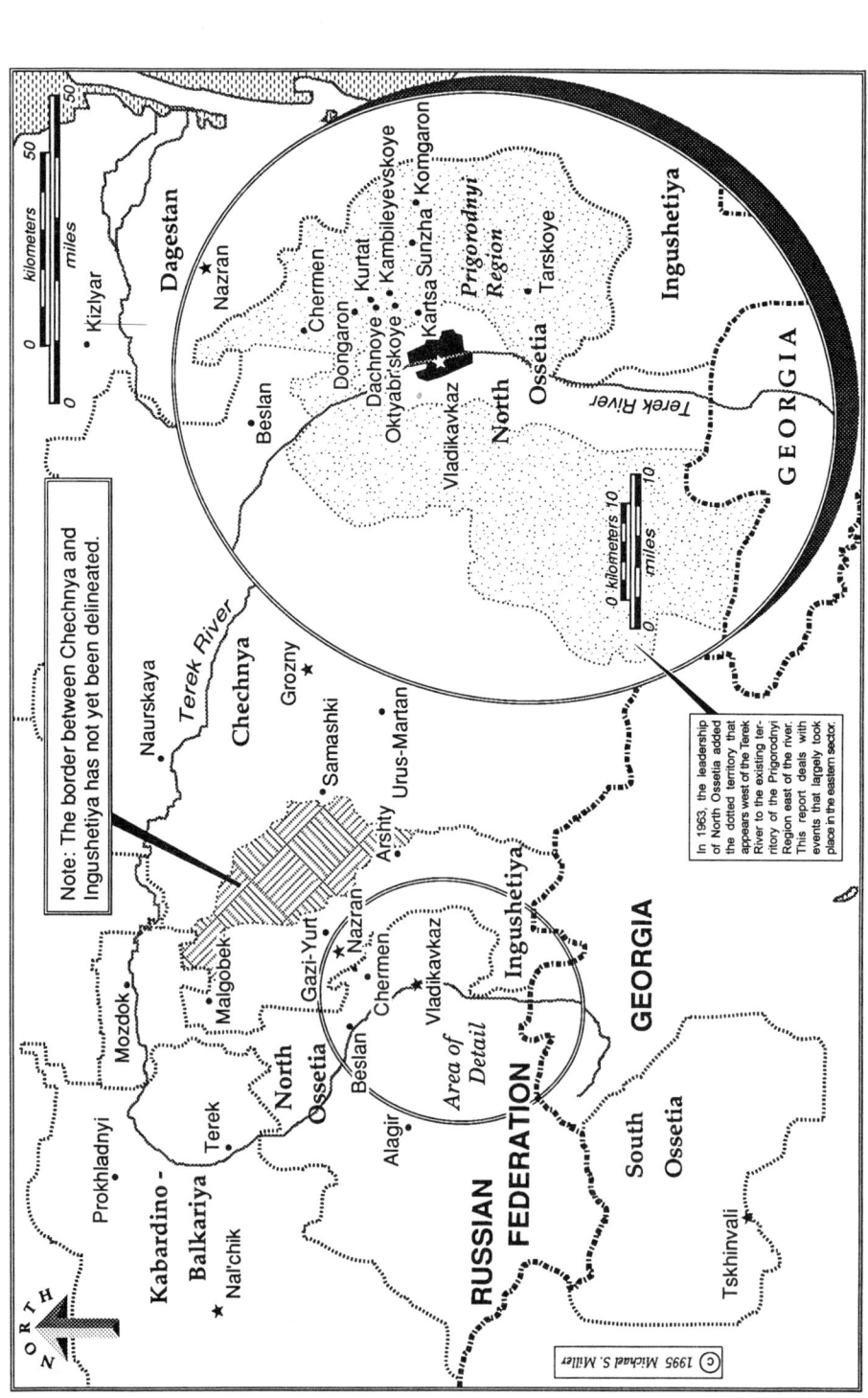

I. SUMMARY AND RECOMMENDATIONS

On October 31, 1992, armed clashes broke out between Ingush militias and North Ossetian security forces and paramilitaries supported by Russian Interior Ministry (MVD) and Army troops in the Prigorodnyi region of North Ossetia, a republic of the Russian Federation located in the North Caucasus. The fighting, which lasted six days, had at its root a dispute between ethnic Ingush and Ossetians over the Prigorodnyi region, a sliver of land of about 978 square kilometers over which both sides lay claim. That dispute has not been resolved, nor has the conflict. Both sides have committed human rights violations. Thousands of homes have been wantonly destroyed, most of them Ingush. More than one thousand hostages were taken on both sides, and as of this writing approximately 260 individuals—mostly Ingush—remain unaccounted for, according to the Procuracy of the Russian Federation. Nearly five hundred individuals were killed in the first six days of conflict. Hostage-taking, shootings, and attacks on life and property continue to this day.

While the present report investigates human rights violations committed by all parties to the conflict from 1992 to the present, its major emphasis is on the events between October 31, 1992 and November 31, 1992, on the process of return for the displaced, and on attempts to bring to justice those who committed criminal acts connected with the conflict. The report also examines the Russian government's weak response to events leading to the armed conflict and its utter failure to prevent the destruction of thousands of homes and dwellings.

The fighting was the first armed conflict on Russian territory after the collapse of the Soviet Union. When it ended after the deployment of Russian troops, most of the estimated 34,500-64,000 Ingush residing in the Prigorodnyi region and North Ossetia as a whole had been forcibly displaced by Ossetian forces, often supported by Russian troops. There are no authoritative figures for the number of Ingush forcibly evicted from the Prigorodnyi region and other parts of North Ossetia, because there were no accurate figures for the total pre-1992 Ingush population of Prigorodnyi and North Ossetia. Ingush often lived there illegally and thus were not counted by a census. Thus the Russian Federal Migration Service counts 46,000 forcibly displaced from North Ossetia, while the Territorial Migration Service of Ingushetiya puts the number at 64,000. According to the 1989 census 32,783 Ingush lived in the North Ossetian ASSR; three years later the passport service of the republic put the number at 34,500. To date, only a small minority of the displaced Ingush have returned to their homes. According to the migration service of North Ossetia, about 9,000 Ossetians were forced to flee the

Prigorodnyi region and seek temporary shelter elsewhere; the majority have returned.

BACKGROUND

Originally part of the Checheno-Ingush ASSR, the Prigorodnyi region was given to North Ossetia in 1944 after Stalin's forced deportation of the Ingush and Chechens from the North Caucasus that same year. When the Checheno-Ingush ASSR was reconstituted in 1957, Prigorodnyi was not returned, and North Ossetian authorities discouraged the Ingush from repatriating there. The Ingush consistently maintained their claim to the territory and their right of return; however, a poorly conceived 1991 law passed by the Russian Federation Supreme Soviet allowing for the return and territorial recompensation of Soviet nationality groups repressed and exiled by Stalin simply acted as a catalyst for the conflict. In 1991 and 1992, tensions between Ingush and Ossetians in the region grew quickly, and there were numerous ethnically motived killings and violent clashes before the ultimate explosion.

The present Ingush-Ossetian emerges from the policies of both Tsarist Russian and Soviet governments, which exploited ethnic differences to further their own ends, namely the perpetuation of central rule and authority. Tsarist policy in the North Caucasus generally favored Ossetians, who inhabited an area astride the strategically important Georgian Military Highway, a key link between Russia proper and her Transcaucasian colonies. In addition, the Ossetians were one of the few friendly peoples in a region that for much of the nineteenth century bitterly resisted Russian rule. Russian authorities also conducted population transfers of native people in the area at will and brought in large numbers of Russian Cossack settlers, thus creating resentment and competing claims for land.

Under the Soviets, local Cossacks were punished for their support of anti-Soviet White forces during the Russian Civil War (1918-1921) and banished from the area, including from the Prigorodnyi region which was given to the Ingush, ostensibly for their support of the Red or Bolshevik forces during the conflict. Soviet administrators often arbitrarily created territorial units in the North Caucasus, thereby enhancing differences by splitting apart like peoples or fostering dependence by uniting different groups. In 1944, Stalin's paranoia led to the forced deportation of the Chechens and the Ingush (among other groups) and the dissolution of the Checheno-Ingush ASSR. The Prigorodnyi region, which had formed part of that unit, was given to North Ossetia, where it remained even after the reconstitution of the Checheno-Ingush ASSR in 1957.

Ossetians were also pawns of central policy. Many ethnic Ossetians living in Georgia and the South Ossetian Autonomous Oblast were told to move to areas in the Prigorodnyi region vacated by the Chechens and the Ingush in 1944. Soviet policy from 1960-1990 generally favored Ossetian attempts to control the Prigorodnyi region and prevent Ingush return. In April 1991, the Russian Federation Supreme Soviet passed the "Law on the Rehabilitation of the Repressed Peoples," which promised the Ingush return of the Prigorodnyi region but created no concrete mechanism to carry this out. Before the break-up of the Soviet Union, some Russian politicians, such as Russian President Boris Yeltsin, were favorably inclined toward the Ingush, who were seen as anti-Soviet and anti-center, i.e. against Soviet President Gorbachev and Soviet central authorities.

Lax or biased attempts by Russian authorities to deal with the conflict since its outbreak in 1992 have blocked its resolution. Few of those who committed the crimes mentioned above have been brought to justice. Russian forces deployed once the conflict broke out are implicated in the forced expulsion of the Ingush population from the Prigorodnyi region. In violation of orders to separate Ingush and Ossetian armed groups and stop the fighting, Russian troops either sat idly by while Ossetian paramilitaries and North Ossetian security forces forced out Ingush civilians along with the fighters, or they assisted those efforts with armor or artillery support. In other cases Russian troops did bring Ingush safely out of the conflict zone, but the question arises why those forces did not carry out their orders and stop Ossetian attempts to force out the Ingush, thus obviating the need to bring the Ingush out of harm's way. Once active fighting ended in mid-November 1992 and the majority of Ingush had been expelled from Prigorodnyi, Russian security forces did little to prevent widespread looting and wanton destruction of abandoned homes in the area.

The Temporary Administration—now the Temporary State Committee—had the task of stabilizing the situation and aiding Ingush resettlement, but it made little use of its wide-ranging powers under the emergency rule decree in force in the Prigorodnyi region and surrounding areas between November 2, 1992 and January 31, 1995. As the supreme executive power in the emergency rule area, the Temporary Administration controlled Interior Ministry (MVD) and army troops and had the power to stop disturbances and protect life and property. But it rarely punished criminal behavior by extremists on either side, especially by armed radical North Ossetian groups, and did little to stop demonstrations. Disarmament of militant groups implicated in human rights violations, while a priority of the Temporary Administration, was carried out haphazardly. A Temporary State Committee with diminished powers was founded by a presidential decree in February 1995 after the state of emergency was not renewed. Its main task was to coordinate the activities of federal authorities in the region, but the Temporary State Committee proved as feckless as its predecessor in bringing about Ingush resettlement or achieving stability and security.

RECOMMENDATIONS

Based on our August 1994 research mission to the Prigorodnyi region, Human Rights Watch/Helsinki makes the following recommendations.

To the North Ossetian and Ingush governments:

- Immediately and unilaterally release all individuals who still may be held as hostages; allow authorities from the Temporary State Committee as well as legitimate Ossetian/Ingush groups to conduct searches for the missing, including searches for possible mass graves;

- Afford every assistance to Russian federal authorities in their efforts to bring to justice those responsible for crimes committed during and after the conflict, and bring to trial those suspected of involvement in criminal activities connected with the conflict;

- Discipline law enforcement bodies that carry out their duties in a prejudicial manner, and try those suspected of involvement in crimes;

- Allow all ethnic groups to reside unhindered on the territories of Ingushetiya and North Ossetia;

- Conduct a public campaign on ethnic reconciliation.

To the Russian government:

- Conduct an investigation into the actions of Russian Army and Interior Ministry (MVD) units concerning the looting and destruction of homes in the Prigorodnyi region;

- Bring to justice those who have committed crimes connected with the conflict;

- Act decisively to carry out Decree #2131 allowing for partial return of Ingush displaced to their homes in the Prigorodnyi region of North Ossetia, and work towards the return of all displaced to their homes.

To the European Community and the United States government:

- Investigate possibilities for funding projects in the Prigorodnyi region of North Ossetia that will aid in ethnic reconciliation and the respect for human rights.

II. DEMOGRAPHY AND ETHNOGRAPHY

According to the 1989 census, the last one conducted before the collapse of the Soviet Union, the North Ossetian ASSR had a population of 632,428, of which 334,876 were Ossetian, 189,159 Russian, and 32,783 Ingush.[1] According to that same census, 163,762 Ingush resided in the Checheno-Ingush ASSR out of a total population of approximately 1.3 million. As of January 1, 1994, Ingush officials put the population of Ingushetiya at 249,830.

Although these figures are out-dated, given the numerous conflicts and forced migrations that have plagued the region, they serve as a baseline for lack of any new, comprehensive census.

An indigenous Caucasian mountain people, the Ingush are Sunni Muslims belonging to the western branch of the Vainakh people and are closely related to the Chechens.[2] The first official division between Chechens and Ingush was made by Russian colonizers during their conquest of the Caucasus in the mid-nineteenth

---

[1] "Natsional'nyi Sostav Naseleniya SSSR Po Dannym Vsesoyusnyi Perepisi Naseleniya 1989," Moscow: *Finansy I Statistika*, 1991, p. 38. The number of Ingush living in North Ossetia in the 1989 census went under-reported because many Ingush lived in the Prigorodnyi region illegally, i.e. without a residency permit.

A daunting array of territorial classifications are used in this report. In the Soviet system, most territorial delineation was based on ethnicity. The highest territorial body was the Union Republic, of which there were fifteen. All became independent countries after the break-up of the USSR. The next highest was the Autonomous Republic, such as the North Ossetian ASSR or the former Checheno-Ingush ASSR. They were subordinated to a Union Republic, and like the Union Republic, were created along ethnic lines. The North Ossetian ASSR and the Checheno-Ingush ASSR were part of the Russian Socialist Federative Soviet Republic. The next ethnically delineated unit was the autonomous oblast such as the Nagorno-Karabakh A.O. in Azerbaijan. It was usually subordinated to a Union Republic, but could be part of an Autonomous Republic or a Krai. The smallest ethnically-based unit was the autonomous Okrug. After the break-up of the Soviet Union, most Autonomous Republics within the Russian Federation, a former Union Republic, became simply Republics of the Russian Federation.

Non-ethnically based territorial units in the former USSR and now in Russia include oblast and krai, which are similar to provinces.

[2] See Ronald Wixman, *The Peoples of the USSR: An Ethnographic Handbook* (Armonk: M.E. Sharpe, 1984), pp. 82-83, and Lars Funch and Helen Krag, "The North Caucasus: Minorities at a Crossroads," *Minorities Rights Group International Report* (London), 1994.

century as a result of the fact that the western clans of the Vainakh (Galgai and Feappi) did not play a large role in Caucasian War of Sheikh Shamil against the Russians while the eastern ones (the Chechens) did. The Russians were the first to make this distinction.

Ossetians are ethnic Iranian Alans and Sarmatians who originally came to the region from Central Asia in the fourth century. Between the ninth and twelfth century they formed a state-like structure south of the Don river and extending to the North Caucasus. They retreated wholly into the Caucasus area after the Mongol invasion in the thirteenth century, mixing with local Caucasian peoples.[3] The have generally had a friendly relationship with Russia, joining the Russian empire voluntarily in 1774.[4] In March 1995, North Ossetia signed an extensive power-

---

[3] See Funch and Krag, pp. 23-26, and Wixman, pp. 151-2.

[4] One commentator has noted that,
> We have seen in the recent history of North Ossetia a devastating series of interconnected problems of enormous significance for such a small territory. In one case the origins of the problem predated the Soviet era, though it was greatly exacerbated by the policies of that period. In other cases, the origins lay squarely in the Stalinist past. Ossetia has indeed derived very mixed benefits from her association with Russia. In a number of ways she had long been a willing pawn of Russia in the area, and had, in a way, been rewarded by being almost alone among her mountain neighbors in not undergoing the traumas of mass deportation. The degree to which she is still Russia's stalking horse in the area, in the latter's disputes with Georgia and Chechnya, is open to question. Nevertheless, this supportive role has now brought its own costs. She has suffered markedly through the South Ossetian refugee problem and the physical destruction of villages and towns in the Prigorodnyi district. It will take a long time for her to adjust to the new realities of power in the post-Soviet Caucasus.

Julian Birch, "Ossetia: A Caucasian Bosnia in Microcosm," *Central Asia Survey* (1995), p. 52. There are numerous theories explaining pro-Ossetian behavior by Russia in October 1992. Many argue that Russia hoped to draw General Dudayev of Chechnya into the conflict in support of the Ingush. Russian forces would then use this as a casus belli to depose the Chechen leader. Some even contend that Russian authorities bolstered Ingush leaders regarding their claim to Prigorodnyi just before the outbreak of the fighting. Others point out that the North Caucasian Military District headquartered in the North Ossetian capital Vladikavkaz had gained new strategic importance as Russia lost bases in Azerbaijan and was faced with conflicts in two of its former Transcaucasian possessions. The military

sharing agreement with the Russian Federation, similar to one signed earlier with Tatarstan.[5] Today about eighty percent of Ossetians practice Eastern Orthodox Christianity and twenty percent Sunni Islam.

Ossetians can be divided into three groups: the Iron, who inhabit the area north of the Caucasian mountains; the Tuallag, who moved south of the Caucasian mountains and came under Georgian influence; and the Digors, who were converted to Sunni Islam in the 17th-18th centuries by the Circassians (Kabards). Those Ossetians who inhabitant South Ossetian are known in Russian as "Kudartsy" after the "Kudar" ravine where they live, while the Digors are referred to as "Digortsy" after the gorge in which they reside.

---

importance of Vladikavkaz and the North Caucasian Military District has only grown since the outbreak of armed conflict in Chechnya in December 1994; recently a new army group, the 58th, was formed and based in Vladikavkaz.

[5]Itar-Tass, Moscow, "Russia and North Ossetia Sign Power-Sharing Treaty," March 23, 1995.

III. BACKGROUND TO THE CONFLICT

DEPORTATIONS UNDER STALIN

During the Russian Revolution many Ingush supported the Communist Bolsheviks, while the Cossacks favored the anti-Communist white armies. Sergei Ordzhonikidze, a leading Bolshevik operating in the North Caucasus, allegedly promised the Prigorodnyi region to the Ingush in return for their support. On March 24, 1919, the Central Committee of the Russian Communist Party (b) passed a decree on "Decossackification," which ordered forcible resettlement of Cossacks from the Prigorodnyi region; when the white armies were finally defeated, entire Cossack-populated villages—including those in the Prigorodnyi region—were depopulated, and Ingush moved back in.

In January 1920, the Autonomous Mountain Soviet Socialist Republic, referred to as the "Mountaineers Republic," was formed, with its capital in Vladikavkaz. Initially, the "Mountaineers Republic," included the Kabards, Chechens, Ingush, Ossetians, Karachai, Cherkess, and Balkars, but it quickly began to disintegrate and new territorial units were created.[6] By July 1924, only the Ossetians and Ingush remained, and that year they were allotted their own autonomous oblasts. In 1924, the Ingush were given their own territorial unit that included the Prigorodnyi region. The right bank of Vladikavkaz served as the Ingush capital, while the North Ossetians had the other side. In 1934, the Ingush were merged territorially with the Chechens; in 1936 this territory was formed into the Checheno-Ingush ASSR with its capital in Grozny. The Prigorodnyi region still remained within the Chechen-Ingush entity.

On Red Army Day, February 23, 1944, all Chechens and Ingush were forcibly deported to Central Asia and the Checheno-Ingush Autonomous Republic (ASSR) was dissolved; its territory, including the Prigorodnyi region, was parceled out among its neighbors. During the first five years of exile, approximately twenty-five percent of deported Chechens and Ingush perished; no one knows how

---

[6] In reality, all these entities had little real power, but instead were administered by the Executive Committee of the North Caucasian region, which until 1934 was based in Rostov-na-Donu and then moved to Vladikavkaz. See, "Chechnia: A Report." *International Alert* (London, England), November 1992, p. 11. Henceforth, "Chechnia: A Report."

many died in transit.⁷ On June 25, 1946, the Supreme Soviet of the RSFSR issued a decree officially abolishing the Checheno-Ingush Autonomous Republic (ASSR), charging that,

> During the Great Patriotic War, when the people of the USSR were heroically defending the honor and independence of the fatherland...many Chechens...at the instigation of German agents, joined volunteer units... and, together with German troops, engaged in armed struggle against units of the Red Army....⁸

Ostensibly, the deportation was punishment for alleged collaboration with the invading German armies, although the Germans never reached Chechen territory. More likely Stalin ordered the deportation as retaliation for yet another uprising that erupted in the hill country of south-eastern Chechnya in 1940, a time when the Soviet Union and Nazi Germany were basking in the friendship of the Molotov-Ribbentropp Pact of August 1939.

INGUSH RETURN TO THE PRIGORODNYI REGION

In late 1956 and early 1957, after heated debate in the highest ranks of the Communist party, some of the nationalities deported *en masse* during World War II were allowed to return to their native areas in newly-restored administrative units.⁹ On November 24, 1956, the Central Committee of the CPSU passed a

---

⁷ Helsinki Watch, *"Punished Peoples" of the Soviet Union: The Continuing Legacy of Soviet Stalin's Deportations*, (New York: Human Rights Watch, September 1991), p. 23. Henceforth, "Continuing Legacy."

⁸ Alexander Nekrich, *The Punished Peoples: the Deportation and Fate of the Soviet Minorities at the End of the Second World War* (New York: Norton and Company, 1978), pp. 91. Henceforth, "Punished Peoples."

⁹ Ibid., p. 151. Opposition arose within the Communist Party, however, to the return of the Chechens and Ingush. The foremost scholar on the deported peoples, Alexander Nekrich, writes that: "Individual party members... tried to argue that it was impossible for the Russian and Chechen-Ingush population to live side-by-side on the territory of the republic, and adopted a negative attitude toward the restoration of autonomy."

decree entitled, "On the Restoration of the National Autonomy of the Kalmyk, Karachai, Balkar, Chechen, and Ingush Peoples." Two months later, the Presidium of the USSR Supreme Soviet passed another edict, "On the Restoration of the Checheno-Ingush ASSR as part of the RSFSR."[10] Taken together, the decrees allowed Chechens and Ingush to return over a four-year period, from 1957 to 1960.

For the Ingush, however, this represented only a partial restoration because the Checheno-Ingush ASSR was reconstituted within slightly altered borders that excluded the Prigorodnyi region. Before their deportation from the area in 1944, Ingush comprised roughly ninety percent of the Prigorodnyi population.[11] To compensate for the loss of the Prigorodnyi region, Soviet authorities added to the Checheno-Ingush ASSR the Kargalinskii, Shelkovksii, and Naurskii regions from nearby Stavropol Krai.[12] It was little consolation to the Ingush that the new territories were much larger than the Prigorodnyi region as they had wanted the return of Prigorodnyi itself. In 1963, North Ossetian authorities changed the borders of the Prigorodnyi region to reduce the Ingush population and increase the Ossetian: Ossetian-inhabited territory on the left bank of the Terek River was attached to the Prigorodnyi region and certain Ingush-dominated villages were transferred to other districts.

The return of the Ingush and Chechens to the newly reconstructed Checheno-Ingush ASSR and to the Prigorodnyi region was further complicated by

---

[10] Ibid., p. 136.

[11] "Zaklyucheniya Komissii Soveta Natstional'nostei VS SSSR po obrashcheniyam Ingushskogo nasileniya, 1990," ("Conclusions of the Commission of the Council of Nationalities of the Supreme Soviet of the USSR by appeal of the Ingush population, 1990.") The commission is also known as the Belyakov Commission. In the Moscow Human Rights Center *Memorial's* excellent report on the present situation in the region, "Cherez dva Goda Posle Voiny: Problema Vynuzhdennykh Pereselentsev V Zone Osetino-Ingushkogo Konflikta," ("Two Years After the War: The Problem of the Forcibly Displaced in the Area of the Ossetian-Ingush Conflict,") Moscow, 1994, p. 17. Henceforth, "Cherez Dva Goda."

[12] The Prigorodnyi region compromised 978 square kilometers; the three regions of Stavropol Kari attached to the Checheno-Ingush ASSR comprised nearly 5,200 square kilometers. Some argue that these three regions—largely inhabited by ethnic Russian descendants of Cossacks—was attached to serve as an ethnic counterweight to the returning Chechens and Ingush. See "Chechnia: A Report," p. 16.

the fact that between 1944 and 1957, 77,000 individuals from North Ossetia, South Ossetia, and Dagestan had been settled—some forcibly—in areas previously inhabited by Ingush and Chechens.[13] Furthermore, Slavs had also settled in the region.

Consequently, Ingush returning to Prigorodnyi were not greeted enthusiastically.[14] There were obstacles to receiving the obligatory residency permit ("propiska"), without which one could not find a home or job in any given town and was subject to administrative sanctions. Land and homes were not returned, and in some cases unpublished decrees from North Ossetian authorities prevented such sales.[15] In 1982, the Council of Ministers of the USSR passed a decree limiting the issuance of residency permits in the Prigorodnyi region and the sale and purchase of homes. While the decree was "ethnically neutral," it overwhelmingly affected the Ingush, since it was they who wanted to return. An Ossetian official admitted that, "In 1982... a decree limited the issuing of *propiski* in the Prigorodnyi region. While the decree was not openly ethnically-based, in fact it was directed against the Ingush, who still sought to come to the area."[16] In 1990, the North Ossetian Supreme Soviet adopted another similar decree limiting Ingush migration to the Prigorodnyi region.

---

[13] Ibid., p. 15. Human Rights Watch/Helsinki interview with Tamerlan Tsoriyev, consultant for inter-ethnic questions, Supreme Soviet of North Ossetia, August 12, 1994, Vladikavkaz, North Ossetia, Russian Federation. Henceforth, Human Rights Watch/Helsinki interview with Tsoriyev. Also, according to Tsoriyev, two decrees of March 7 and March 9, 1944, issued by the Council of Peoples Commissars of the USSR, ordered the forced resettlement of both North and South Ossetians.

[14] Chechens and Ingush returning to Checheno-Ingush ASSR itself also faced discrimination and obstacles. In August 1958, after a fight broke out in a Grozny bar between an Ingush and a Russian sailor, in which the latter was killed, anti-Chechen and Ingush violence broke out. It was stopped with the introduction of troops.

There was also an out-migration of non-Chechen and Ingush from the area to avoid conflict. Soviet authorities chose to relocate 2,574 families to the left bank of the Terek because of the influx of Chechens and Ingush.
See Nekrich, *The Punished Peoples,* pp. 144-166.

[15] "Cherez Dva Goda," p. 16.

[16] Human Rights Watch/Helsinki interview with Tsoriyev.

Ingush from Prigorodnyi commonly resent these restrictions. Ruslan Pliyev, an Ingush official, explained,

> From 1957 on the Ingush people led a constant struggle to return to their homes and their land. Our return was decided upon, but the leadership of North Ossetia did everything to block this. The home where I and my parents were born was not returned. And if an Ossetian tried to sell an Ingush back his home, his Ossetian neighbors threatened him with vigilantism. And they blocked us with residency permits and with discrimination at work.[17]

Ingush from Prigorodnyi also allege job and education discrimination after their return. An Ingush civic leader in Chermen, a village in the Prigorodnyi region, told Human Rights Watch that,

> From the very beginning until today they told us, 'Don't forget that you live in Ossetia'....In the factories and enterprises the directors were Ossetians, the specialists were Ossetians, but the workers were Ingush. A year or two before the conflict there wasn't one Ingush director in the whole Prigorodnyi region and only two specialists...[in 1981] the whole oblast level of the party was dissolved and reformed. A new oblast party committee with a certain Odintsov as its head, a Russian, was formed. With his arrival there was progress, things started to get redone. In those rural areas where the Ingush population comprised sixty to seventy percent of the population the Ingush began to get elected as chairmen of the state farms. In Chermen, Tarskoye, Maiskoye, and Kurtat, Ingush became heads of collective farms. But only after the arrival of Odintsov.[18]

---

[17] Human Rights Watch/Helsinki interview with Ruslan Pliyev, Head of the Ingush Presidential Administration, Nazran, Ingushetiya, August 17, 1994, Henceforth, Human Rights Watch/Helsinki interview with Pliyev.

[18] Human Rights Watch/Helsinki interview with Ayub Matsiyev, August 14, 1994, Chermen, North Ossetia. Henceforth, Human Rights Watch/Helsinki interview with Matsiyev.
All the villages named are in the Prigorodnyi region.

An Ingush woman interviewed by Human Rights Watch charged that her daughter was not allowed to study in North Ossetia because of her ethnicity. "They didn't hire us in jobs or accept our children in educational institutions. My oldest daughter wanted to be a teacher, she got all fives, but we had to go to Grozny for her to study, no one would accept her in North Ossetia."[19]

While bribery was widespread in the former Soviet Union (to gain posts or favors), it seemed to be the only way for Ingush in the Prigorodnyi region to gain any administrative or high level position. One Ingush told Human Rights Watch that,

> At enterprises the practice arose whereby an Ingush had to pay a bribe to occupy a middle-level position. And the Ossetians would speak about this, not hiding anything...If an Ingush did buy a position he would be allowed to work for some time unhindered, but then he would be called to the boss who would tell him, "If you don't resign you will have big problems...." This trend was especially strong from 1987 to 1992. They did this to give the impression that they weren't against all Ingush. They would say your position has become redundant. A month later they would reopen this position and hire an Ossetian.[20]

Most Ossetians generally acknowledge the practice of paying bribes, but claim that in spite of this the Ingush in Prigorodnyi lived as well as or better than the Ossetian population. One Ossetian, for example, told Human Rights Watch that, "The Ingush occupied some good positions, they worked in profitable positions. But they received all this for bribes. They bought these posts. I wouldn't say that the Ingush were in a repressed position."[21]

Relations between Ingush and Ossetians in Vladikavkaz and in the Prigorodnyi region were tense in the 1970s and early 1980s. In 1973, Ingush held demonstrations for four days (January 16-19) on Lenin Square in Grozny, forcing a candidate member of the Politburo, Mikhail S. Solomentsev, to come to

---

[19] All fives is the equivalent of a "straight A" in the United States. Human Rights Watch/Helsinki interview, Nazran, Ingushetiya, August 17, 1994.

[20] Ibid.

[21] Human Rights Watch/Helsinki interview, Vladikavkaz, August 15, 1994.

Chechnya to address the crowd.[22] An Ingush from Prigorodnyi told us that there were meetings in Prigorodnyi itself, which he termed, "the birth of our movement."[23] In October 1981 there were clashes in Prigorodnyi between Ingush and Ossetians, the most serious of which occurred in Vladikavkaz.[24] Ingush blame the Ossetians for instigating the trouble and allege that they had support from Moscow authorities.[25] Ossetians allege Ingush sparked the conflict and claim that one of them killed an Ossetian taxi driver. Crowds attacked government and police buildings in the North Ossetian capitol and armored cars were deployed and a curfew instituted.[26] In January 1982, the North Ossetian first party secretary was replaced by a Russian deemed less biased against Ingush.[27]

NATIONAL TENSIONS INCREASE UNDER PERESTROIKA

As "perestroika" reached its peak in 1990, events in the North Ossetian ASSR, the South Ossetian Autonomous Oblast, and in the Checheno-Ingush ASSR slowly began to spin out of control. Peoples throughout the Soviet Union were rediscovering the "national question," and this region was no exception. Ingush intellectuals began to debate publicly the question of the Prigorodnyi region. Groups such as "Niiskho" (Justice) made the return of Prigorodnyi central to their political platforms, a policy that found general public support.[28] A September 1989

---

[22] Helsinki Watch, *Continuing Legacy,* pp. 48-9.

[23] Human Rights Watch/Helsinki interview with Matsiyev.

[24] "Cherez Dva Goda," p. 17.

[25] Helsinki Watch, *Continuing Legacy*, p. 48.

[26] Birch, "Ossetia," p. 54.

[27] Ibid.

[28] By 1992, Niiskho had radicalized and called for the return of Prigorodnyi by force. See Fiona Hill's excellent study of the present day situation in the North Caucasus, "'Russia's Tinderbox': Conflict in the North Caucasus and its Implications for the Future of the Russian Federation," Harvard University, Strengthening Democratic Institutions Project, September 1995, p. 14.

conference of Ingush intellectuals and nationalists decided to reestablish an Ingush territorial unit within the RSFSR which had existed until 1934 when Ingushetiya was merged with Chechnya.[29] In 1989 and 1990 60,000 signatures were gathered supporting that demand.[30] In March 1990, an article in *Pravda* perceived by the Ingush as denying their claim to the Prigorodnyi region provoked almost a week of demonstrations that reportedly drew 10,000 people. Consequently, the USSR Supreme Soviet created the "Belyakov Commission" to investigate Ingush demands. The commission concluded that Ingush claims to the Prigorodnyi region were not unfounded.[31]

The year 1991 witnessed almost continual demonstrations and counter demonstrations by Ingush and Ossetians. In March 1991, Ingush rallied in the present Ingush capital of Nazran for the restoration of an Ingush state within its pre-1934 borders, and there were reports that Ingush tried to seize Ossetian homes in Prigorodnyi.[32] On March 24, 1991, Boris Yeltsin spoke at a rally in Nazran and supported the restoration of an autonomous Ingush republic.[33] The rally sent a USSR People's Deputy, Kh. Fargiyev, to present Ingush claims to the North Ossetian ASSR Supreme Soviet. Fargiyev called for the restoration of Vladikavkaz, the North Ossetian capital, as the Ingush capital; the rescinding of the ban on issuing residency permits for the Prigorodnyi region; an end to the settlement of South Ossetian refugees in the Prigorodnyi region; and the establishment of a commission to pay damages to Ingush who were deported in 1944.[34] North Ossetia authorities rejected these demands. Ossetians responded in kind with their own

---

[29] Helsinki Watch, *Continuing Legacy*, pp. 48-49. Following information from this report unless otherwise cited.

[30] Birch, "Ossetia," p. 54.

[31] Ibid., p. 48.
A summary the commission issued stated that the legal rehabilitation of the Ingush had not been achieved; that the issue should be investigated by the RSFSR Supreme Soviet; that the 1982 limitation on residency permits in the Prigorodnyi region should be abolished; and that for practical purposes the right bank of Vladikavkaz could not become the Ingush capital. See also "Cherez Dva Goda" and footnote 11.

[32] Birch, "Ossetia," p. 55.

[33] Ibid.

[34] Helsinki Watch, *Continuing Legacy*, p. 50.

"First Congress" of the Ossetian peoples, held in July 1991. The congress condemned extremist Ingush and rejected any border changes.

On April 19, 1991, at least one person was reported dead and several others were wounded during a clash that broke out between Ingush and North Ossetian police in a village in Prigorodnyi. The next day, the North Ossetian ASSR Supreme Soviet responded by declaring a state of emergency in the Prigorodnyi region and in Vladikavkaz.[35] One thousand five hundred Russian Ministry of Interior troops were dispatched to the region, but they stopped neither the rallies nor the violence. On April 28, 1991, three Ingush driving through the Cossack village of Troitskoye were pulled from their car and beaten; in the fight that ensued, eight were killed and twenty-four wounded.[36] In June 1991, a "First Congress" of the peoples of the Chechen-Ingush Republic repeated demands concerning Prigorodnyi. In September 1991, in another visit to the area, Yeltsin hinted at support for Ingush claims to Prigorodnyi, but this could have been a move to split the Ingush from the restive Chechens who eventually declared the independence of Chechnya in November 1991.[37] In October 1991, the North Ossetian Supreme Soviet and Council of Ministers appealed to the USSR and Russian Federation Presidents, stating that an "extraordinary socio-political situation had developed" and calling on central authorities to intervene.[38] In November thousands of Ingush rallied again for the creation of an Ingush republic and expressed anger at the sluggishness in resolving the territorial problem with the North Ossetian ASSR.[39]

---

[35] "State of Emergency in Vladikavkaz; Violence in South Ossetia," BBC Monitoring Service, April 21, 1991.

[36] Helsinki Watch, *Continuing Legacy*, p. 49.

[37] Birch, "Ossetia," p. 55.

[38] "North Ossetia Fears Ingush Aggression," BBC Monitoring Service, October 11, 1991.

[39] "Supporters of Ingush Republic Stage Rally in Nazran," BBC Monitoring Service, November 9, 1991.

LAW ON THE REHABILITATION OF REPRESSED PEOPLES

On April 26, 1991, the RSFSR Supreme Soviet passed the "Law on the Rehabilitation of the Repressed Peoples," which promised territorial redress for the Ingush as well as other minorities deported by Stalin.[40] Unfortunately, the law set out no concrete mechanism for its realization; it represented a decent if ill-conceived legislative attempt in the last few months of the Soviet Union to rectify Stalin's crime of nearly a half-century earlier. The drafters of the law would have had to perform a tight-wire act to restore the rights and territories of the repressed peoples without upsetting the status quo or affecting the rights of those presently residing in those areas. Unfortunately, the drafters failed miserably: they provided no means for bringing about a transfer of territory or compensating those who lived on territory to be returned.

Article 3 states only that,

> The rehabilitation of the repressed peoples signifies the recognition and realization of their right to the restoration of the territorial integrity of their homeland existing before the anti-constitutional policy of forced recarving of borders, to the restoration of national-state formations existing before their dissolution....
>
> Rehabilitation of the repressed peoples also entails the return of peoples not having their own national-state formations in accordance with their wishes to their places of traditional residence on the territory of the RSFSR.

---

[40] Between 1941 and 1944, the Kalmyk, Karachai, Kurds, Balkar, Chechen, Ingush, Volga German, Meskhetian Turk, and Crimean Tatar peoples were deported *en masse* and with great loss of life to barren areas in Central Asia. In 1937, the Koreans living in the Soviet Far East suffered the same fate. In 1956 Khrushchev rehabilitated the "repressed peoples," but not all were not allowed to return to their homes. Moreover, certain territories previously allotted to these ethnic groups were either not reconstituted (the Crimean Tatars and the Volga Germans) or were reformed but within altered borders (Checheno-Ingush Autonomous Republic, minus the Prigorodnyi district). The law also envisioned rehabilitation of ethnically-Slavic Cossack groups, wom the Bolshevicks had repressed during the Civil War and in the early 1920s because of their military service to the Tsars.

Background to the Conflict

> *In the process of the rehabilitation of the repressed peoples the rights and lawful interests of citizens presently residing on the territory of the repressed peoples should not be infringed upon.*[41]

Further complicating matters, Article 6 allows for the law's implementation to be postponed, and indeed a moratorium had been in effect until July 1, 1995, on resolving territorial disputes.[42] The moratorium had been adopted at the urging of Russia's Security Council, which feared the laws destabilizing effects. When the moratorium expired in 1995, it was extended until 1997.[43]

The law's lack of clarity drew criticism from an unpublished Russian government report on the Ingush-Ossetian conflict that was leaked to the press in 1994.[44] Vladimir Lozovoi, present head of Moscow's Temporary State Committee in the region, criticized in particular the law's lack of implementation mechanisms. Lozovoi told Human Rights Watch that,

> By itself, the law on the territorial rehabilitation of the repressed peoples was humane. And if someone says that this law was not

---

[41] "Law of the Russian Soviet Federative Socialist Republic on the Rehabilitation of the Repressed Peoples," April 26, 1991. Author's italics.

[42] Inna Korobova, "Law on Exoneration is a Political Bluff," *Moscow News* (Moscow), no. 49, December 6-13, 1992. Article 6 states that "in necessary instances a transitional period could be instituted."

[43] Petr Pliyev, "North Caucasus: A Sad Anniversary: Three-Year-Old Events Have Not Become History," *Nezavisimaya Gazeta* (Moscow), October 27, 1995, p. 3 FBIS-SOV-1995, p. 69.

[44] See for example, a government report entitled "Idei I Lyudi: Politicheskaya Otsenska (Proyekt) Soveta Bezopasnosti Rossiiskoi Federatsii obstoyatel'stv vooruzhennogo Konflikta na territoriyakh Severo-Osetinskoi SSR: Ingushskoi Respubliki v oktyabre-noyabre 1992 goda," ("Peoples and Ideas: A Political Evaluation [Draft] of the Security Council of the Russian Federation on the Circumstances of the Armed Conflict on the Territory of the North Ossetian SSR and Ingush Republic in October-November 1992,") *Nezavisimaya Gazeta* (Moscow), March 23, 1994, p. 5. The Russian Security Council approved the draft, but it was not made public. It was released to the press in early 1994 by Sergei Shakhrai, then Minister for Nationality and Regional Policy Affairs and former head of the Temporary Administration. Hereafter, "Draft Political Evaluation."

> necessary, it just isn't true, that is another extreme. It simply was passed without the corresponding mechanisms for realization. Back then, in 1957, it wasn't complicated to make part of Stavropol Krai part of another republic....This law was like a time bomb.[45]
>
> Pertaining to territory, the President of Russia put a moratorium on all territorial changes. We think it should be extended. Because to decide such issues in the Caucasus is not only impossible but undesirable and dangerous.

The Ingush contend that the law itself is good, but that North Ossetia's militant behavior made it a dead letter in the Prigorodnyi region. Ruslan Pliyev, the head of the presidential administration in Ingushetiya, charged that

> The events of October and November 1992 were the armed expulsion of the Ingush population from the territory of North Ossetia. [These events] by their very nature were a carefully planned act by the leadership of North Ossetia to prevent the implementation of the Law on the Rehabilitation of the Repressed Peoples.... The National Ingush Council (Narodnyi Sovet Ingushetii) did an awful lot so that the law on rehabilitation would be passed. It constantly worked in Moscow, it had a lot of contacts.
>
> As soon as the law about rehabilitation was published in 1991, in North Ossetia, it was "bayonetted." There was a negative propaganda campaign on all levels against the law....The North Ossetian leadership presented everything that went on here [in support of the law] as though the Ingush were preparing aggression. As though a danger hung over North Ossetia. All this was done to justify the deployment of armed formations, the

---

[45] Human Rights Watch/Helsinki interview with Vladimir Lozovoi, former head of the Temporary Administration, Deputy Prime Minister, Russian Federation, Vladikavkaz, North Ossetia, August 16, 1994. In February 1995, Lozovoi became head of the Temporary State Committee, which replaced the Temporary Administration when emergency rule was lifted. Hereafter, Human Rights Watch/Helsinki interview with Lozovoi.

OMON, the National Guard, and armed self-defense units. And parallel with this, military hardware was purchased.[46]

For their part, the Ossetians fear that the law was aimed at stripping Prigorodnyi away from their republic and was directly responsible for the outbreak of the conflict. As one official remarked,

> Many things point to the fact that if there had not been this political preparation....these events would hardly have occurred on such a scale and with such consequences. I mean the scale of military operations and the death of so many people. But why do we think this way. We, for example, see the reason. It's the passing of the law on the rehabilitation of repressed peoples of April 26, 1991.[47]

A top Ossetian official in Chermen, where Ossetians suffered more than in any other village in Prigorodnyi, also blamed the armed conflict on the law: "All this was provoked by the law on the rehabilitation of the repressed peoples. It wasn't worked out down to the details and everyone could interpret it as he wished. After this law [was passed], people started to hold demonstrations. They said that Russia had given land, but that the Ossetians refused to give it up. The Ingush had their 'informal' organizations."[48]

Although the Ingush generally insist that it was the non-implementation of the law that created the problem, some admit that certain "hot heads" stirred passions. One official in Nazran, the Ingush capital, told Human Rights Watch that,

> [After the law was adopted], the further chain of events was as such: Several different hotheads demanded the quickest realization of the law, there were all different types of demands, and in Prigorodnyi they were sometimes very provocative. In

---

[46] Human Rights Watch/Helsinki interview with Pliyev.

[47] Human Rights Watch/Helsinki interview with Tsoriyev.

[48] Human Rights Watch/Helsinki interview, village of Chermen, North Ossetia, August 15, 1994.

several cases we're sure that there were calls made by provocateurs, especially sent there.[49]

BREAKAWAY OF CHECHNYA AND THE CREATION OF THE REPUBLIC OF INGUSHETIYA

In November 1991, seven months after the adoption of the Law on the Repressed Peoples, the Checheno-Ingush ASSR unilaterally declared independence from Russia as the Republic of Chechnya-Ichkeriya. The three Ingush-inhabited regions of the Checheno-Ingush ASSR decided not to join Chechnya in its independence drive precisely for fear that this would jeopardize its chance to reclaim the Prigorodnyi region.[50] On June 4, 1992, the Russian Supreme Soviet founded the Republic of Ingushetiya within the Russian Federation, but without defined borders. The Ingush believed that the ultimate borders of the new republic would still include the disputed territory of Prigorodnyi, as provided for in the Law on the Rehabilitation of Repressed Peoples.[51] At the same time Ossetian officials, concerned that the newly-formed republic would seek to include the Prigorodnyi district, successfully lobbied for a five-year moratorium on the law's implementation; then vice-chairman of the North Ossetian ASSR Supreme Soviet, Yuri Biragov, commented that, "Ossetia is pleased by any law that does not envision redrawing her border."[52]

Since all the central structures that exercised power and authority over the three Ingush regions of the Checheno-Ingush ASSR remained in Grozny, the capital of the newly formed Chechen Republic, the traditionally under-developed Ingush territories were left utterly leaderless. One Ingush from Chermen told us that,

---

[49] Human Rights Watch/Helsinki interview, Nazran, Ingushetiya, August 17, 1994.

[50] The three largely Ingush-populated regions of the Checheno-Ingush Autonomous Soviet Socialist Republic (ASSR) were the Nazran, Malgobek, and Sunzha regions. Many descendants of Cossacks also lived in the Sunzha area.

[51] Lyudmila Leont'eva, "Chto dlya Ingushetii Nezavisimost, to dlya Dudayeva Provokatsiya," ("What's independence for Ingushetiya is a provocation for Dudayev,") *Moskovskiye Novosti* (Moscow), no. 25, June 21, 1992, p. 9.

[52] Ibid.

> For a year and a half Ingushetiya remained without any authorities; Chechnya broke away...A demonstration could remove any chairman, any council. During this time almost every day [Ingush sent] telegrams to the Russian Supreme Soviet and to the President himself requesting them to stop this. National movements were rather strong at this time. [But our telegrams] had absolutely no effect....The Russian authorities for eighteen months left Ingushetiya without any functioning authority. Regional soviets and other structures worked in name only.[53]

Vladimir Lozovoi, head of the former Temporary Administration and presently chair of its successor, the Temporary State Committee, seconded this opinion:

> The Ingush Republic was formed inside the borders of three administrative regions of the former Checheno-Ingush ASSR. But to this day the borders of that republic [Ingushetiya] are not defined. And that is what exploded. Imagine, on the one hand, the law on the repressed people was not realized, and on the other hand, a new republic [Ingushetiya] was formed spontaneously. And when all this combined together, there were provocateurs who pushed people to bring the law into effect through force.[54]

This lack of authority proved disastrous once armed conflict broke out in October 1992. One Ingush reflected,

> All national movements were sick with this [Ingush-Ossetian] conflict. And the Ingush national movement is no exception. And when the conflict started, part of the leadership simply

---

[53] Human Rights Watch/Helsinki interview, August 14, 1994, Chermen, North Ossetia.

[54] Human Rights Watch/Helsinki interview with Lozovoi.
After the fighting subsided in December 1992, Major General Anatolii Chaikovski of the Internal Troops of the Russian Interior Ministry complained that, "The absence of authorities in Ingushetiya complicates restoring order and the rule of law." See, "Armiya v ochage Konflikta," ("Army in the Heart of the Conflict,") *Rossiiskiye Vesti* (Moscow), November 12, 1992, p. 1.

stepped aside and let the masses take their course. There and then, when it was necessary to say this is not right, this is wrong, they didn't have the authority, the boldness. And the mass became uncontrollable."

THE ROLE OF SOUTH OSSETIANS IN THE CONFLICT

As a result of a war in the South Ossetian Autonomous Oblast (A.O.), which is part of Georgia, thousands of South Ossetian refugees were forced out of their homes in both the South Ossetian A.O. and in Georgia proper and fled to North Ossetia. There some of them played a significant role in both the tension that led to the fighting, in the fighting itself, and in the destruction that followed. These ethnic Ossetian refugees—many of whom settled in the Prigorodnyi region—created new economic and demographic problems for an already creaking social infrastructure in the North Ossetian ASSR and competed with Ingush for jobs.[55] As of mid-1994, 43,168 Ossetian refugees lived in North Ossetia, most

---

[55] This was not the first group of Ossetians from Georgia and the South Ossetian A.O. to come involuntarily to North Ossetia and Prigorodnyi. In 1944, Ossetians from both Georgia and South Ossetia were forcibly moved to the Prigorodnyi region to occupy homes and farms abandoned by the deported Ingush and Chechens. Many of the new refugees from South Ossetia were going to seek shelter with relatives who had arrived in 1944. A sixty-year-old Ossetian man who has lived in the village of Tarskoye in the Prigorodnyi region since 1944 was originally from South Ossetia. He explained that, "I moved here in 1944, we were forcibly moved here. They told us, 'Go, there are empty villages there.' We were forcibly resettled. Many were." Ossetians generally claim that since Stalin's deportations victimized these South Ossetians as well as the Ingush, they should not be forced to move from the Prigorodnyi region. One North Ossetian official stated that,

> They [the Ingush] say they left here [Prigorodnyi Region], and we say you were given three other regions [as compensation]. And in the place of the Ingush here [in 1944] came Ossetians from South Ossetia, whom the Georgians kicked out you can say. Ingush went from here...and in their place Ossetians. They've lived here already fifty years--we're not returning anyone. They're here since 1944...Half of our territory is mountains, you can't grow wheat there, you can't build factories....

Human Rights Watch/Helsinki interviews, Tarskoye, North Ossetia, August 19, 1994; Vladikavkaz, North Ossetia, August 13, 1994.

from Georgia. Of these, 16,000 lived in Prigorodnyi.[56] South Ossetian militias played a significant role in the wanton destruction of Ingush homes after open hostilities ended on November 5, 1992.

Between 1989 and 1992, fighting flared in the South Ossetian A.O. and in Georgia between ethnic Ossetian paramilitary troops and Georgian Interior Ministry (MVD) units and paramilitaries.[57] South Ossetia had demanded to secede, and Georgia cracked down on the renegade area by sending in troops. Approximately 100,000 ethnic Ossetians fled Georgia and South Ossetia, and another 23,000 Georgians headed in the other direction. One hundred villages were reportedly destroyed in South Ossetia. Also the North Ossetia-Georgian border went largely uncontrolled, providing an almost unhindered access point for weapons, fighters, and ammunition. in both directions.[58]

North Ossetians and others with whom we spoke stated that the South Ossetian refugees found it difficult to adapt to conditions in North Ossetia in part because of their traumatic deportation and their more traditional culture. A Russian journalist in June 1992, four months before the outbreak of the conflict, commented that,

> Considering the psychological trauma connected with the effort to survive of Ossetians from Tskhinvali, [the capital of the South Ossetian A.O.] the situation is tense in the extreme. Large numbers of refugees...are in a state of despair. They can blow up at any cause.[59]

---

[56] See "Cherez Dva Goda," pp. 30-31.

[57] For more information into this conflict see, Helsinki Watch, *Bloodshed in the Caucasus: Violations of Humanitarian Law and Human Rights in the Georgia-South Ossetia Conflict* (New York: Human Rights Watch, 1992). Figures and information cited on the South Ossetia conflict come from this report unless otherwise noted.

When Soviet authorities founded the "Mountaineers Republic" in 1920, Ossetians living on the northern slope of the Caucasian range, i.e. " North " Ossetians, received a territorial unit within it. Ossetians living on the southern slope, i.e. "South" Ossetians, were given an autonomous oblast within Georgia in 1923.

[58] "Draft Political Evaluation," *Nezavisiymaya Gazeta,* p. 5.

[59] Leont'eva, June 21, 1992, p. 9.

In addition, it quickly became apparent that the South Ossetian refugees would not be short-term refugees. A Russian sociologist who lives and works in Vladikavkaz told us that,

> There were so many refugees from South Ossetia that there were even problems between local Ossetians and those who had come, because many of them...are marginal. They are more Georgian by their way of life, mentality, by everything. Our government had the idea that all the refugees (from South Ossetia) would one day return. And when we did an opinion poll, we [learned] that the majority of people who remained here are from internal regions of Georgia....They experienced [there] some physical threat or violence. And no one or nothing can force them to return there. They live here in dormitories in the worst of conditions, but they have accepted life in those conditions rather than return. They believe there still is a risk for them.[60]

Tensions grew between South Ossetian refugees and the roughly 15,000 ethnic Georgian citizens of North Ossetia. A deputy to the North Ossetian Supreme Soviet explained,

> When the war began in South Ossetia [Georgia], there were thousands of refugees....Naturally, those Ossetian refugees from South Ossetia and from Georgia who fled here wanted to kick out Georgians living here. There are 15,000 Georgians living here, just in Vladikavkaz...We stopped this, no one fled.[61]

---

[60] Human Rights Watch/Helsinki interview with Yelena Fedosova, consultant on Cossack questions, Institute of Sociology, Vladikavkaz, North Ossetia, Russian Federation, August 16, 1994.

[61] Human Rights Watch/Helsinki interview with Vyacheslav Magometovich Lagkuyev, North Ossetia, Russian Federation, August 15, 1995. Henceforth, interview with Lagkuyev.

Ossetians, however, generally agree that the South Ossetians must be accommodated and given the same treatment as Ingush displaced from Prigorodnyi.[62]

South Ossetian leaders openly boast about their role in the fighting, and South Ossetian paramilitaries, militia, and some South Ossetian refugees are implicated in much of the wanton destruction and violence committed during and after the outbreak of hostilities in 1992. The deputy chairman of the South Ossetian Supreme Soviet, Alan Chochiyev, commented that, "In the course of the military conflict in the Prigorodnyi region the Ossetian people for the first time came out as one....the events in the Prigorodnyi region were, for the first time in recent history, a military-national appearance of the Ossetians."[63] Oleg Teziyev, commander of the notorious South Ossetian Battalion, angrily rejected the North Ossetian government's limited attempts at reconciliation with the Ingush:

> I accept the laws of those who fight. You can argue if they are "dirty" or they are "clean," but those are the rules. Either I accept [them], or I reject them and become a refugee... Imagine: the south [Ossetia] is destroyed, Prigorodnyi is lost....I don't understand how one can vote for a leader who calls for war with the Ingush, and now wants his people to live peacefully with them. [Imagine:] a leader, who with all his power cursed Adeamon Nykhas, Chochiyev, and me, and then terrified and

---

[62] One Ossetian official told us that, "I have to say that on the territory of North Ossetia there is a huge number of refugees and displaced of all nationalities. But for some reason the main attention goes to the Ingush. Things connected with refugees have to be worked out in a 'complex solution.' A refugee, whether from South Ossetia, Georgia, or Prigorodnyi, is a refugee and has to be given the same treatment." Human Rights Watch/Helsinki interview with Sultan Kabolov, North Ossetian government official, assistant chairman of the committee on nationality questions, Vladikavkaz, North Ossetia, Russian Federation, August 19, 1994. Hereafter, Human Rights Watch/Helsinki interview with Kabolov.

[63] Yevgenii Kurtikov, "Sobytiya v Prigorodnom Raione prodemonstrirovali Voenno-politicheskoye Yedinstvo Osetin," ("The Events in the Prigorodnyi region demonstrated the political-military unity of the Ossetians,") *Nezavisimaya Gazeta* (Moscow), January 5, 1993.

pale called Tskhinvali [the South Ossetian capital] and asked for help.[64]

In some cases North Ossetians tried to protect Ingush, while South Ossetians attacked them. While a North Ossetian neighbor hid and helped an Ingush family interviewed by Human Rights Watch, South Ossetian refugees looted their home, and a policeman originally from South Ossetia torched the remains.[65]

Another Ingush man who was held hostage complained that, "The 'Kudartsy' [South Ossetians] were the worst. When they exchanged us, 'Irontsy' [North Ossetians] came to escort us. It was easier with them, they didn't swear at us or insult us."[66]

An Ossetian intellectual explained—but did not justify—the behavior of South Ossetians by pointing to their own humiliation and degradation at the hands of Georgians during the Georgian-Ossetian conflict in 1992:

> The South Ossetians played a large role in forcing out the Ingush. They are often accused in the press of having exhibited a certain violence and cruelty (*zhestokost*). The war was very cruel. But what was the situation then of the South Ossetians? They were ripped apart by the Georgians, Tskhinvali was surrounded, it was fired upon at point-blank range. It's not only the war. They were morally degraded. Of course they were very angry.[67]

---

[64] "Moi Narod bili za to, v chem on ne vinoven," *Demokraticheskaya Ossetiya* (Vladikavkaz, Russian Federation), no. 11-12, August 1994, p. 1. The South Ossetian Battalion took part in fighting in the conflict and acquired a reputation for brutality.

[65] Human Rights Watch/Helsinki interview, Zavodskii Refugee Camp, Nazran, Ingushetiya, August 18, 1994. See sections, "1992-1994: Violations of the Rules of War in the Ingush-Ossetian Conflict," and "Zavodskii (A Suburb of Vladikavkaz): Violations by Ossetian Forces."

[66] Ibid.

[67] Human Rights Watch/Helsinki interview with Vladimir Dzarasov, economics professor, head of Ossetian civic group called "Civil Position," Vladikavkaz, August 16, 1994. Henceforth, Human Rights Watch/Helsinki interview with Dzarasov.

In August 1995, an Ingush official charged that over seven hundred residences in the Prigorodnyi region that had belonged to Ingush had been seized by South Ossetians.[68]

THE ARMING OF OSSETIANS AND INGUSH

During the three years preceding the outbreak of conflict in October 1992, both the Ingush and the Ossetians armed at a furious pace. Much of the North Ossetian ASSR's acquisition of weapons was connected with the war in South Ossetia. Weapons flowed into Ingushetiya freely from Chechnya, and until the outbreak of the conflict one could purchase automatic weapons freely at the market in Nazran. Ingush groups of twenty or thirty to two hundred fighters armed with automatic rifles, light machine guns, and rocket-propelled grenades operated in many of the Ingush villages in Prigorodnyi.[69] An Ingush man from Kurtat complained to Human Rights Watch that the Ingush had only light weapons while the Ossetians had heavy weapons such as APCs and artillery.[70]

In 1991, the North Ossetian ASSR Supreme Soviet adopted several decrees incorporating paramilitary groups into North Ossetian security forces. Many of these units had armored personnel carriers and heavy machine guns. One source puts the number of these forces at five thousand.[71] A Russian government report on the conflict describes these decrees in great detail.[72] While the laws and decrees contradicted both North Ossetian law and Russian Federation laws, central authorities did little to stop the process. On November 15, 1991, the Supreme Soviet of North Ossetian ASSR passed the "Law about Supplementing the Constitution of the North Ossetian ASSR," which provided for the creation of

---

[68] Moscow INTERFAX, Foreign Broadcast Information Service, Central Eurasia, August 9, 1995, p. 34.

[69] "Cherez Dva Goda," p. 54.

[70] Human Rights Watch/Helsinki interview, Nazran, Ingushetiya, Russian Federation, August 1994.

[71] Birch, "Ossetia," p. 55.

[72] "Draft Political Evaluation," *Nezavisimaya Gazeta* (Moscow), p. 5. The following information comes from this report.

self-defense forces for the republic as well as of a so-called republican guard. On May 21, 1992, a special session of the North Ossetian ASSR Supreme Soviet adopted a decree that ordered the republic's self-defense committee to produce weapons at enterprises within Vladikavkaz. An attack on South Ossetian refugees by Georgian gunmen in South Ossetia supposedly elicited this measure. In June 1992 the procuracy of North Ossetia raised legal objections to these decrees, but the protest was ignored. Moreover, on October 20, 1992, the "Law On Security" came into force in North Ossetia, allowing for security forces to include local popular self-defense units and the republican guard.

Weapons for a peace-keeping battalion in South Ossetia and for USSR Interior Ministry (MVD) units serving in South Ossetia found their way into private hands. Also, in the fall of 1991, twenty-one BRDM-2, a light armored personnel carrier, were acquired by the directorate of the Prigorodnyi region collective farms. Such armored personnel carriers became commonly known as "collective farm APCs."[73] Although the cannons and machine guns had been removed from them, an examination after the fighting indicated that they had been used in battle.[74] Also, on the eve of the conflict, twenty-four BTR-80 APCs were delivered to the North Ossetian Interior Ministry. Once the conflict broke out, Russian authorities disbursed weapons to North Ossetian authorities, which then found their way into the hands of both militias and North Ossetian Interior Ministry (MVD) units.

---

[73] In Russian it was called a "Kolkhoznyi BTR."

[74] "Draft Political Evaluation," *Nezavisimaya Gazeta* (Moscow), p. 5.

IV. 1992: TENSIONS AT A BOIL

Throughout 1992, tension, crime and ethnically-motivated attacks grew between Ingush and Ossetians in the Prigorodnyi region. A leaked Russian report noted the ethnic nature of crimes and attacks in the Prigorodnyi region:

> The criminal situation in the republic—almost all of which had an ethnic angle—deteriorated in the nine months preceding the conflict in Vladikavkaz and in the Prigorodnyi region. Efforts to investigate these crimes were haphazard and ineffective. During this period there were thirty one premeditated murders, thirteen serious assaults, 120 bandit attacks, and 135 robberies, of which sixteen murders, one hundred bandit attacks, and sixty-nine robberies went unsolved.[75]

Ossetians and Ingush interviewed by Human Rights Watch confirmed that relations between the two had steadily deteriorated throughout 1991 and 1992. An Ossetian official in Chermen, for example, ticked off alleged crimes by Ingush against Ossetians: "Tensions existed already for quite some time. Two years before the conflict broke out, at least. Armed men appeared on the kolkhoz [collective farm] field and would steal equipment. Our taxi drivers were killed there. By 1991 Ossetians stopped going to Ingush villages. It already was unsafe. On eight different occasions Ingush stole equipment from the state farm in Chermen." Another Ossetian in Chermen commented on the mutual mistrust between Ossetians and Ingush: "[Before the conflict] they were together all the time at work; they would close the door and speak in Ingush, insulting [us]. We work together, different nationalities, you should speak in Russian, the lingua franca. But they spoke in Ingush."[76] A retired Ossetian woman from Kurtat remembers that relations in the village between the Ingush and the Ossetians deteriorated before the conflict broke out, with Ingush insulting the Ossetians by

---

[75] Ibid.

[76] Human Rights Watch/Helsinki interview, village of Chermen, North Ossetia, Russian Federation, August 15, 1994.

calling them "Beria's Whores."[77] In July 1992, the North Ossetian deputy interior minister stated that 290 police were guarding farm workers in the Prigorodnyi region from conflict with Ingush.[78]

Ingush tell similar stories of mistrust and recriminations. Lyuba, a fifty-five-year-old Ingush women who lived in Dachnoye, commented that, "You know before this started we were always threatened—they told us that we had occupied their land. At work the Ossetians would harass us and when they drank on the job they would shout, 'Get out, Prigorodnyi Raion [region] is ours!'"[79] According to Ibragim Kosboyev, a member of the Russian parliament from Ingushetiya,

> If one wants to discuss the prelude to the conflict, you just have to remember that in the eighteen months [before the conflict broke out], while there was a state of emergency, twenty-five Ingush were killed by people in uniform—Ossetian guardsmen and OMON members. No one was punished....[80]

By October 1992, the situation in the Prigorodnyi region had reached its peak. All sides were heavily armed. There was no central authority in Ingushetiya, but rather a hodge-podge of regional councils. North Ossetia, flooded with ethnic Ossetian refugees from Georgia, perceived itself under threat from the east [Ingushetiya] and the south [Georgia]. Furthermore, North Ossetian security agencies in Prigorodnyi did not act as impartial guardians of public order but as another partisan militia. An Ingush we interviewed in October 1992 remembers a general unease, a feeling that a conflict was growing with the Ossetians. He relates that, "Several times, I don't remember the exact date, several Ingush guys were killed [by Ossetians] and an Ingush girl was crushed by an APC. You could feel that a conflict was close, but no one wanted this. But the authorities didn't take

---

[77] Lavrenti Beria, like Stalin a Georgian, became head of the NKVD, the forerunner of the KGB, in December 1938. He was executed in 1953 shortly after Stalin's death. He oversaw the deportation of the Chechens and Ingush—among others—in 1944.

[78] BBC Monitoring Service, July 30, 1992.

[79] Human Rights Watch/Helsinki interview, Gaziyurt, Ingushetiya, Russian Federation, August 17, 1994.

[80] Sergei Karkhanin and Aleksandr Iskandaryan, "Ne Strelyat' !," ("Don't Shoot!") *Rossiiskiye Vesti* (Moscow), November 12, 1992, p. 1.

1992: Tensions at a Boil

any steps." He said that all sides had weapons, including automatic rifles, but that the Ossetians had heavy weapons such as APCs and artillery and were organized in self-defense, guard, and OMON units.[81] By the last week of October, sporadic shoot-outs and clashes between Ossetian police and Ingush militants erupted. This resulted in the Ingush construction of barricades around their neighborhoods and villages. North Ossetian authorities demanded the removal of these barricades and the disarmament of all Ingush.

CHRONOLOGY OF THE EVENTS IMMEDIATELY PRECEDING THE ARMED CONFLICT

The following is a rough chronology of the events of October 21-30, 1992, preceding the eruption of open hostilities on October 30, 1992.

October 21-22, 1992

- Clashes broke out in the village of Yuzhny, leading to six deaths, including two Ossetian policemen. The police had gone to the village to investigate an incident, and a clash broke out with local residents.[82] Ingush allege that a total of six Ingush were killed in the Prigorodnyi region between October 20-22, including an eleven-year-old girl crushed by an Ossetian armored personnel carrier.[83]

October 24-26, 1992

- On October 24, 1992, a session of the Nazran, Malgobek, and Sunzha regional councils and Ingush deputies from the Prigorodnyi region of North Ossetia was held. This body decided to organize self-defense units that would patrol all areas in the Prigorodnyi region where Ingush resided. The decision stated that,

---

[81] Human Rights Watch/Helsinki interview, Gaziyurt, Ingushetiya, Russian Federation, August 17, 1994. OMON are special police units similar to a mix of a SWAT team and riot police.

[82] "Six Killed in Southern Russian Shootout," *Reuters*, Moscow, October 23, 1992.

[83] Human Rights Watch/Helsinki interview with Pliyev.

> ....the position of the Ingush in the Prigorodnyi region of North Ossetia continues to worsen, and in the past years has become dangerous for human life....Such a situation is possible given the fact that repressing, insulting, and destroying the Ingush has become state policy of the leadership and parliament of North Ossetia....The government of Russia has not taken the necessary measures to realize laws reinstating the constitutional rights of the Ingush people to their state and territorial unity....[It is decided] to unite volunteers in self-defense units and organize their patrols [*dezhurstvo*] in all population centers in the Prigorodnyi region of North Ossetia where Ingush live. The service of [self-defense] units will exist until land taken away by the Stalinist regime is returned to the jurisdiction of the Ingush Republic...in order to ensure the security of the volunteers and of Ingush living in the Prigorodnyi region, [the decree] allows the use of personnel and other weapons, state transport and other technical services....[84]

- Over the next several days Ingush residents of the Prigorodnyi region set up barricades blocking the entrance to their villages.

- The Supreme Soviet of the North Ossetian ASSR ordered the removal of all barricades from villages and the disarming of all Ingush. If this were not done, the North Ossetian ASSR government would begin combat operations with the participation of the republican guard and popular militias.

---

[84] "Resheniye Ob'edinennoi sessii Nazranovskogo, Malgobekskogo, Sunzhenskogo Raisovetov Narodnykh Deputatov Ingushskoi Respubliki I Deputatskoi Grupy Prigorodnogo Raiona Severnoi Osetii," ("Decision by the Unified Session of the Nazran, Malgobek, Sunzha Regional Councils of the People's Deputies of the Ingush Republic and the Deputies' Group of the Prigorodnyi Region of North Ossetia,") Nazran, October 24, 1992.

1992: Tensions at a Boil

- On October 26, 1992, the Presidium of the Russian Supreme Soviet ordered the creation of a mixed commission to deal with the mutual Ingush-Ossetian problems.[85]

October 28, 1992

- Ingush allege that two Ingush brothers were killed by an Ossetian armored personnel carrier; in response, the Ingush rebuilt barricades to their villages and armed themselves.[86]

October 30, 1992

- Fighting breaks out in the evening in the villages of Kurtat, Dachnoye, Oktyabr'skoye, and Kambilevskoye between Ingush and Ossetian armed groups.[87]

October 31, 1992

- Armed Ingush from Ingushetiya enter the village of Chermen and attack the police station. The Ingush also disarm a unit of Russian Interior Ministry (MVD) troops there and seize several armored personnel carriers.[88]

---

[85] "Cherez Dva Goda," p. 18.

[86] Human Rights Watch/Helsinki interview with Pliyev. Pliyev told Human Rights Watch, "Then the Russian authorities intervened [October 26], said everything would be okay, that there would be no more abusive behavior or shootings, and the Ingush population took away their posts...But things continued, and on October 28, two more Ingush were killed, and the people again rose and closed all the entrances and exits to their villages. Galazov, the North Ossetian leader, again made the same demand (to remove the armed posts), but we refused..."

[87] "Cherez Dva Goda," p. 18.

[88] One Ingush deputy admitted that the Ingush had launched the attack on Chermen first. He stated that, "And there arose a revolt—unplanned, not organized by anyone, Ingush self-defense groups went over the border to the Prigorodnyi region, which, according to the Law on the Restoration of the Rights of Repressed Peoples, should be returned to Ingushetiya."

VI. 1992-1994: VIOLATIONS OF THE RULES OF WAR IN THE INGUSH-OSSETIAN CONFLICT

The conflict in the Prigorodnyi region of North Ossetia can be divided into two stages: October 31-November 5, 1992; and November 6, 1992 through the present. The overwhelming majority of violations occurred during the first period, as the result of armed clashes between Ingush militias on one side and North Ossetian Interior Ministry troops, North Ossetian paramilitaries, and South Ossetian armed groups on the other. Russian Interior Ministry Troops and army units sent to the region ostensibly to restore order helped North Ossetian forces defeat the Ingush armed groups, often leading assaults. As a consequence, the vast majority of Ingush living in the Prigorodnyi region of North Ossetia, between 34,500 and 64,000 people, were forcibly displaced. Some 9,045 Ossetians fled their homes also, but by mid-1994 about two-thirds had returned.[89]

During the first period of the conflict, North Ossetian Interior Ministry troops and paramilitaries, South Ossetian armed groups, and Ingush militants took hostages, committed murder, looted, wantonly destroyed civilian property, and used indiscriminate fire. All sides also committed these same abuses, albeit to a much lesser degree, during the second stage of the conflict. Russian forces often stood by and allowed these events to occur, and in some cases took an active part in some, such as looting. There were also reports that Russian forces used indiscriminate fire against civilian areas in actions against Ingush militias.

During the second period, a majority of Ingush homes in the Prigorodnyi region were looted by North Ossetian paramilitaries and South Ossetian armed groups again with—at the very least—the acquiescence of North Ossetian and Russian security authorities. Most of this destruction occurred in the second two weeks of November 1992 and early December in spite of the fact that a state of emergency had been proclaimed in November 2, 1992, and the Prigorodnyi region was largely under the control of Russian and North Ossetian forces by November 5, 1992, after the Ingush had fled or been expelled. The state of emergency was annulled in February 1995. As a result of the conflict, a total of 2,728 Ingush and

---

See Karkhanin and Iskandaryan, "Ne Strelyat,'" p. 1.

[89] Ingush never left the village of Maiskii, and shortly after the fighting ended slowly started to trickle back to Kartsa and Chermen. Most other villages inhabited by Ingush remain abandoned, and no Ingush live in Vladikavkaz, North Ossetia's capital, which had been before October 31, 1992, home to approximately 17,000 Ingush.

848 Ossetian homes as well as numerous schools, shops, restaurants, and various parts of the infrastructure were destroyed.[90] Half of the destroyed Ossetian homes have been fully repaired.

According to the Russian Federation Procuracy, between October 31 and November 5, 1992, 583 were killed (350 Ingush/192 Ossetians), 939 individuals were wounded (457 Ingush/379 Ossetians), 261 were reported missing (208 Ingush/37 Ossetians), and 1093 were taken hostage (708 Ingush/289 Ossetians).[91]

Hostage-taking began almost immediately after open hostilities commenced and exchanges began almost immediately after the fighting stopped. Hostage-taking has continued to a much lesser degree to the present. On November 9, 1992, ninety people, among them sixty men, were sent to Ingushetiya from North Ossetia. Usually women and children were the first to be exchanged since most men were suspected of having taken part in the conflict, though security officials had insufficient physical evidence to prove this. In the first full week after the conflict ended on November 5, 1992, most of the hostages were exchanged, according to figures from the former Temporary Administration. At that time it was believed that 310 Ingush and 180 Ossetians were still being held hostage. An additional seven Russian military personnel were believed imprisoned by the Ingush.[92] At present there are still 196 Ingush and thirty-seven Ossetians reportedly missing.[93]

---

[90] "Cherez Dva Goda," pp. 21-2. All information on destroyed homes and village populations comes from this source unless otherwise cited.

Many of the Ossetian homes were destroyed when Ingush militants controlled certain towns and villages in Prigorodnyi region (especially in Chermen) in the first few days of the conflict. But some Ossetian homes were looted and destroyed by South Ossetians, who were outsiders who did not know which house belonged to whom.

[91] Ibid., pp. 18-19. The Temporary Administration gives slightly different figures for dead. See section, "Official Russian Casualty Figures."

[92] Georgii Melikyants, "Rossiiskiye voiska voshli v Ingushetiyu I kontroliruyut situatsiyu V Severnoi Osetii," ("Russian forces enter Ingushetiya and control the situation in North Ossetia,") *Izvestiya* (Moscow), November 11, 1992, p. 1.

[93] "Cherez Dva Goda," p. 18.

DACHNOYE

Violations by Ossetian Forces

Lyuba, a fifty-five-year-old Ingush woman, lived in Dachnoye, a predominantly-Ingush village about five kilometers northeast of Vladikavkaz. Of the 418 homes in Dachnoye, 390 belonged to Ingush and eleven to Ossetians; all but two were fully destroyed. The last time Lyuba saw her husband, Musa Magomedovich Kh., was on November 2, 1992, when she and others fled the village. She has not heard of or from her husband since that time. Her home was looted and burned. According to Lyuba,

> The firing started on Saturday, October 31, from the direction of Vladikavkaz. All night it continued, increasing in force by the next morning. The Ossetians were moving to surround the village, their APCs were already visible. My husband told me, "It's time for you to go."[94]

Her husband stayed at home because, according to Lyuba, the family had cattle, and they were afraid they would lose them if everyone left. She heard reports that he was taken hostage on November 4, 1992 but has heard nothing since.

CHERMEN

A farming village, Chermen lies about ten kilometers north of Vladikavkaz on the road to Nazran, the Ingush capital. It is another four or five kilometers to the Ingush border. Chermen's 7,500 inhabitants were divided almost equally between Ingush and Ossetians, with the former slightly predominating. Ingush lived at the south and north ends of the village, with Ossetians residing in the center. Since the conflict ended, some Ingush have moved back to the northern neighborhood. In the southern end of the village, however, Ingush homes remain empty and ruined because people are afraid to move back. Of Chermen's 1,412

---

[94] Human Rights Watch/Helsinki interview, Gaziyurt, Ingushetiya, Russian Federation, August 17, 1994.

homes, 445 Ingush homes were partially or fully destroyed as were 202 Ossetian dwellings.[95]

Ossetians suffered more in Chermen than in any other place where fighting broke out in October 1992. While few Ossetian homes were destroyed in a majority of the villages of the Prigorodnyi region, in Chermen a third of all Ossetian homes were either fully or partially destroyed. In addition, many were killed by Ingush fighters or taken hostage during the 1992 fighting.

According to most accounts, armed Ingush militants attacked the militia post in Chermen early on the morning of October 31, 1992, and killed the police inside. At some point that morning Ingush fighters disarmed several Russian soldiers and seized their armored personnel carriers.[96] There were reports that Ingush fighters arrived on Kamaz trucks—large, heavy-duty commercial Soviet vehicles—that specifically had been fitted with armor plating. Ingush fighters held the village or parts of it until November 4, 1992, during which time they looted and destroyed homes, took hostages, and reportedly summarily executed at least two individuals. On or around November 4, 1992, units of the Russian army--with Ossetian Interior Ministry (MVD) troops and paramilitaries in their wake--retook the village. After the village was recaptured, Ingush were killed, taken hostage, abused, and their homes were looted and destroyed. While Russian forces did not take hostages—though their indiscriminate fire may have killed civilians—they did little or nothing to stop the actions of the Ossetian forces. Half of all Ingush homes in the village were destroyed, and the southern half of the settlement, where Ingush predominated before the conflict, stands empty, looted and destroyed.

Violations by Ingush Forces

Human Rights Watch spoke with Kazbek, a fifty-five-year-old Ossetian who lives in Chermen and had worked as a cook at the village cafe. During the conflict, his parents were taken hostage and his home looted and destroyed. At 8:00 A.M. on October 31, 1992, he headed out to dig potatoes in the collective farm fields; before he reached there, however, his son caught up with him and announced, "A war has started." He remembers on that day that,

---

[95] There were also 18 homes owned by Russians, three of which were destroyed and two belonging to families of other nationalities, both of which suffered no damage.

[96] Russian Interior Ministry troops had been posted near the village since a state of emergency was declared in early 1991.

> We could see armed Ingush on Kamaz trucks that had been fitted with armor. They were coming from the direction of Nazran...At about noon we started to evacuate people to Olginskoye.[97] As we were going there people were shooting at us. The next day my parents were taken hostage, Tugan Kh. and Vera Kh. My mother is seventy, my father died last year. My mother was exchanged after two days of captivity, my father, after eight.[98]

Around November 8, 1992 (after Russian forces secured the village), he returned to his home, which had been destroyed and looted. According to Kazbek:

> My house was destroyed on November 2 or 3, 1992. Those who stayed told me that Ingush were in my home three or four hours [looting], they took all that was good and then torched the place...they did that to about every third house....[Those who stayed] told me that groups went down the street, and local Ingush pointed out where an Ossetian lived. The looters, however, were outsiders. It was planned. One or two looted the house, another drove livestock away, a third would set the place ablaze. There was a foundation and some walls when I returned, not much else.

Zinaida Ivanovna A., age fifty-six, lived with her family in Chermen where she worked more than twenty years at a small cafe. She reports that she was taken by Ingush militants and held for nine days in Nazran. Just prior to her captivity, she witnessed looting and the killing of an unarmed male Ossetian hostage held by Ingush militants. Zinaida, who was later exchanged, states that,

> It started on a Saturday, October 31, 1992. They herded some Russian soldiers to our village. They had come on APCs, but the Ingush had detained them at the bridge and stripped them of their uniforms....The Ingush put on their uniforms and cordoned off the crossroads. It was our turn to take the kolkhoz's animals to pasture that morning, a relative came to our house and said,

---

[97] Olginskoye, an Ossetian village, lies just to the west of Chermen across a river.

[98] Human Rights Watch/Helsinki interview, Chermen, North Ossetia, Russian Federation, August 14, 1994.

'Don't take the animals out. Something horrible is happening outside.' There were so many gathered there, in Kamaz trucks, in ambulances, in APCs. All armed....There were some local Ingush and Ingush from Nazran.

On Sunday, November 1, they [Ingush] started to loot cars and machinery from the state farm. On Saturday they had already seized the state farm building and blocked it off. They also started to fire wildly on Sunday....About forty of us were sheltered in the courtyard of a neighbor on Ostrovskaya street. We stood there and saw the Ingush firing at everything and burning houses. Around 11:00 A.M. on Sunday, the Ingush started to go house to house and take hostages. One of them came in the courtyard [where we were hiding], he was holding a grenade. Children started to cry. He shouted, 'If you don't be quiet, I'll blow you up.'

Then they started to take the men out. One of them, however, Arshak Kuliyev, hid behind a door but they found him. They placed him against the door and began to fire, hitting his legs. He couldn't stand, he was on his knees, and he began to crawl behind the door. They started to drag him in another room, hitting him with their rifle [butts]....Then they fired into him. Then two guys dragged him out of the house, cut his eyes and slashed his body. Then they brought some water, washed their knives, and put them back in their pockets as if nothing had happened.

They said that they wouldn't harm the women and children after they took away the men. I went to see what was going on in the street, and an armed Ingush shouted at me, 'Come on, get out and come here quickly or I'll shoot everyone.' We walked out along the road, then they put us in cars and took us away....[99]

Tamara S., age forty-seven, claims that she was also taken hostage on November 1, 1992. She and her family made an initial attempt to flee on October

---

[99] Human Rights Watch/Helsinki interview, village of Chermen, North Ossetia, Russian Federation, August 15, 1994.

31, but they turned back to their home after seeing that Ingush had blocked the road south leading towards Vladikavkaz. She lived in the middle of Chermen. Tamara explains that,

> Those who were still left in the village gathered together. It had become impossible to leave. Everything was blocked off and we started to think of what to do. I had hid my children in our house. Then I noticed by our house a small truck had stopped, one armed fighter got out and shouted to his friends, "Get out, this house." He was pointing to my house. When I saw that I ran towards my house--my children were inside--and shouted: "Don't shoot." They swore at me. They weren't Ingush, but mercenaries, Chechens. I could tell by the way they spoke and later I asked one...They shouted at me, "Where is your son? Where is your husband?" I told them and they took my husband away in the small truck. An APC they took from the Russians came up; on it sat an Ingush electrician in the village, Mukharbek M. I screamed at him how he could be doing this. They then started to loot the home, ripping through things and taking what they wanted. After that another armed fighter threw two grenades in the house, but neither went off.

According to Tamara, all the Ossetian houses on Mayakovskii street were looted:

> They opened drawers and wardrobes, pulled things out and tossed them about. They took clothes, a stereo, [and] a television. One put on my daughter's coat. I told him he should be ashamed, it was a women's coat, but he growled at me, "Don't you think I have a daughter?"

The next day, she was taken hostage along with her sister-in-law, Gabet S., and two of her neighbors, a husband and wife. They were reportedly taken to Nazran, where they were brought to the police station and registered. The men and women were separated. She was held with forty-six other people in her cell. After six days she was released, and traveled to Olginskoye, where she found her children. Her husband, she believes, was murdered by Ingush; his corpse was discovered on January 27, 1993. He had been shot in the back of the neck. Mrs. S. also alleges that Murzabek Tukayev, an old man, was killed after his wife was taken hostage because he was too old and immobile.

Tamerlan is a forty-six-year-old Ossetian who lived with his extended family in Chermen all his life. His home was totally destroyed as a result of the fighting, though no one from his family was killed or taken hostage. In late 1993 he managed to make partial repairs to his house to allow his family to occupy a part of it. He told Human Rights Watch that he is categorically against the return of any Ingush.[100]

In August 1994, Vitalii Karayev was the head of the administration of the village of Chermen. During the fighting his home was reportedly destroyed and looted by Ingush fighters, and his father, brother, and mother were taken hostage. He reported that the same fighters murdered his neighbor, Ruslan Khavkazov.

> My brother, mother, and father were taken hostage. A neighbor was murdered. This happened on October 31. When people started to flee, when the houses started to burn, everyone began to head in the direction of the neighboring village Olginskoye. My family and neighbor were stopped by Ingush on the road towards Olginskoye. They hit my father, Sergei, age sixty-two, in the head, and he lost consciousness. They slashed my brother, Anatolii, age thirty-eight, with a knife, and shot and killed our neighbor, Ruslan Khavkazov, also thirty-eight. They took them away in our own car, which they then stole....They were returned on November 8, 1992. There was a list of hostages held there and I found them on it. My house was completely looted. Only an old couch was left. The roof of my house remained, but nothing was left inside. They broke all the windows, but luckily it wasn't torched.[101]

Karayev also reported that the Ossetians in the village still suffer Ingush violence. On August 13, 1994, he alleged that Ingush militants tried to take hostage Aslamov Khariton, a sixty-year-old man who was working in the fields on a tractor. He explains that, "Four men on horses speaking in Ingush rode up to him and tried to grab him. But people ran over and scared them away."

---

[100] Human Rights Watch/Helsinki interview, Chermen, North Ossetia, Russian Federation, August 14, 1994.

[101] Human Rights Watch/Helsinki interview with Vitalii Karayev, Chermen, North Ossetia, Russian Federation, August 15, 1994.

Violations by Ossetian Forces

About half of the 738 Ingush homes in Chermen were completely destroyed as a result of the conflict. Another sixty-five houses were partially destroyed. An Ingush man with whom Human Rights Watch spoke evacuated his family on November 3, 1992. When he left his home at the end of that day it was still standing and in good order. On November 5, 1992, he bribed a Russian soldier to let him through a checkpoint. He explains that, "My home was still burning. We had just pulled up to the house when someone started to shoot at us. We hurried back in the car and drove away."[102]

In the period after November 5, 1992, to the present, the unofficial Ingush representative in the village, Ayub Matsiyev, alleges that thirteen Ingush were murdered in or around Chermen by Ossetian paramilitaries, militants, or security forces.[103] Human Rights Watch was not able to confirm independently all of these allegations. He reports that his own nephew, Bashir Khamidovich Matsiyev, was killed in Chermen at the crossroads on January 20, 1993, and that an additional twelve individuals were killed during this period, including the following:[104]

- Mr. Galakhov, January 1993.

- Four members of the Ivloyev family, allegedly murdered by Ossetian militiamen in February 1993. They went to the village after the Temporary Administration allowed Ingush back in. They were reportedly detained by Ossetian paramilitaries near the village cafe. Their bodies were found later.

---

[102] Human Rights Watch/Helsinki interview, Chermen, North Ossetia, Russian Federation, August 15, 1994.

[103] Human Rights Watch/Helsinki interview, Chermen, North Ossetia, Russian Federation, August 14, 1994.

[104] The head of the police in Chermen, an Ossetian, disputes these figures and alleges that no Ingush were killed in the village and counters that in 1993 three Ossetians were killed in Chermen and one was missing.
   Data from the Procurator and Interior Ministry of Ingushetiya indicates that at least three Ingush were kidnaped in Chermen and four killed.
   See "Cherez Dva Goda," p. 46

- Kurkiyev A.L. and Khaukhayev V.D., in April 1993. They went to cut hay near the border with Ossetia and were allegedly detained by Ossetian paramilitaries and taken away. Their corpses were later discovered.

- The Artskhanov brothers, in June 1993. They came back to the village to look at their house and were murdered.

- Gorikov, Alikhan and Mirzoyev, S.I., in July 1993.

- Sharsudin Yangiyev, in September 1993.

- Mutaliyev, N.I., in December 1993.

Human Rights Watch spoke with the relatives of the Artskhanov brothers, who were allegedly murdered in Chermen on June 18, 1993. The men had gone back to look over the house they had abandoned and were killed by local Ossetians.[105] Their house was not in the Ingush part of the village, but in the Ossetian. A relative lamented that,

> Around 4:30 P.M. [on June 18, 1993], they set out to check their home [in Chermen]. Probably they were followed and quickly captured....They left on the 18th [of June], and the next day they were already in the morgue. They both were killed quickly [after they arrived in Chermen]. If you could have seen what state they were in. No person could withstand it....They took their car and cut both their throats.

KARTSA

Violations by Ossetian Forces
Kartsa, a suburb of Vladikavkaz, lies to the northwest of the city, just down the road from the Russian military base *Sputnik* . On October 24, 1992,

---

[105] Human Rights Watch/Helsinki interview, Maiskii, North Ossetia, August 14, 1994. Maiskii , a predominantly Ingush village, is in North Ossetia and officially belongs to it. *De facto*, however, Ingush authorities seem to have responsibility for its administration.
Maiskii did not experience fighting during October/November 1992, though the few Ossetian families living there and some Russians left.

Ingush militants set up posts around the village; by October 31, 1992, the village, in which Ingush fighters still held positions, was subjected to indiscriminate fire from rifles, machine guns, and grenade launchers by Ossetian security forces and paramilitaries. Many residents fled during the initial fighting to *Sputnik*, sometimes helped there by Russian troops. Other Ingush civilians were killed in crossfire, and at least seven Ossetians who had been taken hostage by Ingush militants were murdered. While most of Kartsa's pre-conflict population of 10-12,000 people were Ingush, currently only about 1,500 remain.[106] Another three hundred or so members of other nationalities, including a handful of Ossetians, also live there.[107] Of the roughly one thousand homes in Kartsa—handsome one- and two-story brick and stone dwellings with fancy tin roofs—one-quarter were wantonly destroyed by Ossetian militiamen, many believed to be from South Ossetia. Many homes were also looted. Other homes were spared destruction because Russian troops quickly set up posts in the village. A favorite method of destruction was to turn on the cooking gas and then spray the home with small-arms fire.

At present, the Ingush in the village are isolated and must apply to the Russian authorities several days in advance to leave the village with an escort. In the past Ossetians have interfered with these convoys, including one hostage-taking incident in 1994 that is dealt with in this report. The need to travel to Nazran is extremely inconvenient for the villagers, especially for medical emergencies. The Ingush in Kartsa must travel to Nazran, about thirty minutes by car, for medical care rather than visit the hospital in Vladikavkaz, five minutes away.

Zakrei Magomedovich Musiyev, an Ingush, still lives in the settlement of Kartsa. He works as an adviser for community relations to the former Temporary Administration and serves as the chairman of the social council of the residents of Kartsa.

Mr. Musiyev lived through the attacks of November 1992, returning to the village after about two weeks. He has lived there ever since. He reported to Human Rights Watch that sixty individuals, mostly civilians, were killed by Ossetian militiamen from October 31 to November 4. Of these, two were Russians and one was Georgian; the rest were Ingush. He alleged that no one from the village

---

[106] Human Rights Watch/Helsinki interview with Zakrei Magomedovich Musiyev, village of Kartsa, North Ossetia, Russian Federation, August 13, 1994. Information concerning background on Kartsa comes from Mr. Musiyev unless otherwise attributed. Mr. Musiyev lived in Vladikavkaz, but was forced out of his apartment by North Ossetian militiamen on October 31 and went to Kartsa, where his mother lived.

[107] "Cherez Dva Goda," p. 38.

1992-1994: Violations of the Rules of War in the Ingush-Ossetian Conflict

participated in the fighting, though it seems clear that armed Ingush fighters were in the settlement. The overwhelming majority of this destruction occurred after the fighting had ended and people had left the village. According to Mr. Musiyev, most people were killed as they fled:

> Ossetian forces surrounded the village. For three days it was like being in a sack. From October 31 to November 3 there was heavy firing from all types of weapons. From the evening of November 3 people started to leave the village....Some went through the fields towards Dachnoye, and some who couldn't go that way—there was heavy fire from Vladikavkaz and Dachnoye...went to [Sputnik], the military base.[108]....Most of these people were killed in the village as they fled to the military base, going from house to house and from street to street. When the APCs came, all the noise, so many vehicles, you can't imagine. You had to hide. Whoever came upon them head-on was shot at point-blank range. There were corpses lying about the streets....Most of the people were killed on the fourth of November.

About four thousand of Kartsa's inhabitants made it to the nearby military base *Sputnik*, where they resided about two weeks. Every day convoys of *Ikarus* buses evacuated Ingush to Kartsa, but some people refused to go and returned to their village at the end of November.

Lida, age thirty-five, lived in Kartsa until the fighting forced her out of her home, which was then wantonly destroyed by Ossetian militiamen. She now lives in a school converted into a refugee center in neighboring Ingushetiya.[109] On the evening of October 30, 1992, Lida reported hearing firing, but thought it was a military exercise; when she woke up the next morning, however, her neighbor told her, "A war has begun." She explains that,

---

[108] If one travels north from Kartsa, he passes through a corridor with Vladikavkaz on the west and Oktyabr'skoye and Dachnoye to the east. Once past Dachnoye, the Ingush border lies about eight kilometers to the northeast, mostly through open land.
    See map.

[109] Human Rights Watch/Helsinki interview, Gaziyurt, Ingushetiya, Russian Federation, August 17, 1994.

> We all sat in the cellar of a neighbor, several families, men, women, and children. We sat there until Monday, but when things would quiet down we would return to our home for a bit and eat. On Monday our elders decided that we should send the children to the Russian military base nearby, and the military came for the kids. The next day the APCs came. They were Ossetians, they were speaking in Ossetian. They stopped by the house and shot at it. We thought they would come in and find us, but they did not. The house started to burn, but the Ossetians left and some of the young men went upstairs to put the fire out.

The remaining people in the cellar wanted to make their way to Nazran, the capital of Ingushetiya, by heading east through the fields, but they heard that Ossetian forces were blocking the way. The following night, Russian forces from the Sputnik military base evacuated them. They spent roughly ten days there, and then were taken in a column of buses to Nazran.

Another Ingush women still vividly remembers the events of 1992 when she and her neighbors were trapped in "a ring of fire." She fled her home with her family on November 2 to the army base at Sputnik, and returned after several weeks to find her house burned to the ground and most of her possessions looted. According to her,

> The firing started on the 30th of October. From Oktyabr'skoye.[110] Then they started to fire from the children's home across the street. We were in a ring of fire....we ran away in the clothes we had on, that's it. They took or destroyed everything.[111]

Since then, the woman has received one small payment from the Russian government and infrequent International Committee of the Red Cross (ICRC) packages as compensation.

All nationalities suffered in Kartsa in November 1992. Grisha, a sixty-five-year-old Georgian, worked in a store in Vladikavkaz and lived in Kartsa. He left his home on November 2, 1992, because of heavy machine gun and rocket fire

---

[110] A largely Ossetian village north of Kartsa.

[111] Human Rights Watch/Helsinki interview, Kartsa, North Ossetia, August 13, 1994.

he claims came from local North Ossetian OMON troops. According to Grisha, "I didn't see any Ingush fighters. The firing was heavy, and I made my escape out the back through the garden. I left everything, and they destroyed it all."[112] He says he received 29,000 rubles in compensation from the Russian government in 1992, and nothing from it since, though the ICRC has helped out with food.[113]

Violence against the Ingush population of Kartsa by Ossetian paramilitaries continues to this day, including the taking of six hostages on May 19, 1994.[114] The incident occurred at 1:30 P.M. on the Chermen road as the six individuals were on their way to Nazran under the escort of an officer of the former Temporary Administration, Lt. Col. Yu. P. Gorev.[115] Four passenger cars filled with automatic riflemen blocked the car, then escorted it to the headquarters of the UOONKH in the Lenin district.[116] When Lt. Colonel Gorev went upstairs to talk to the commander, the car with its occupants was whisked away, and the car was later found abandoned. The procurator of the Lenin district of Vladikavkaz opened a criminal investigation according to Article 126, part II of the Russian Criminal code, and two suspects were identified, though they went into hiding. On May 25, 1994, the commandant of Kartsa received a note from the alleged hostage-takers offering to exchange them for three Ossetian hostages—including a North Ossetian

---

[112] Human Rights Watch/Helsinki interview, Kartsa, North Ossetia, Russian Federation, August 13, 1994.

[113] About twenty-nine U.S. dollars at the time.

[114] The following information comes from two sources: the wife of one of the hostages, interviewed by Human Rights Watch/Helsinki in Kartsa on August 13, 1994; and a press-release issued by the Temporary Administration on May 29, 1994, "Return the people, punish the criminals" ("Vernut' lyudei, pokarat' prestupnikov").

[115] The names and birth dates of the six Ingush taken hostage are as follows: Aldagonov, Isa Magomedovich, b. 1951; Yevloyev, Magomed Albastovich, b. 1922; Albagachiyev, Edolgirei Musiyevich, b. 1937; Khodziyeva, Lidiya Muratovna, b. 1977; Bogotyrev, Akhmet Savarbekovich, b. 1970; Bekova, Tseina Tugaevna, b. 1934.

[116] "UOONKH" is the Russian acronym for a North Ossetian paramilitary group that is supposed to have been disbanded. It stands for "Upravleniye Okhrany Ob'ektov Narodnogo Khozyastva" (Directorate for Guarding Objects of the National Economy). See section seven, "Reconciliation and the Return of Displaced."

Militia Colonel—taken on March 30, 1994.[117] On May 26, 1994, a suspect in the crime, a member of the Lenin District UOONKH, was murdered.

Abdurashid, a middle-aged chauffeur, lived in Kartsa most of his life. He had a residency permit, and reported that his relations with his non-Ingush neighbors, such as Armenians and Ossetians, were fine. Abdurashid's handsome two-story home was totally looted in November 1992, and in early August 1994, an explosive device, probably dynamite, was thrown against the side of his house, blowing out all the windows on one side. He stays mostly in the confines of Kartsa, afraid to venture into Vladikavkaz, a few kilometers away. According to Abdurashid,

> I left for ten days after all the fighting started [in 1992]. It all began with the law to rehabilitate [repressed people] of 1991. A Russian commander, Savvin, came here in November. After he left the BTR's came through shooting, and I left with my family. On the next street over a man, Alaotdin Khadjiev was killed, and another guy, Maksharib, is still missing. When I returned most everything had been taken, and they burned the inside of my house. The few animals we kept were dead in the courtyard.[118]

He came back after ten days and slowly tried to rebuild his home, but in early August 1994 unidentified attackers bombed it: "They threw dynamite at my house--there was an explosion, but no fragments. Until the end of 1993, there used to be posts of Russian troops [Interior Ministry] in the village, but then they took them away. Investigators from the Temporary Administration came, took statements, looked over the damage, and made their report."

---

[117] The note read as follows: "To the head of the temporary administration Lozovoi V. The hostages are alive. They will be exchanged only for the Tebiyev group. Other variations are not acceptable. Six persons of Ingush nationality from the village of Kartsa for three people of the Tebiyev group."

[118] Human Rights Watch/Helsinki interview, village of Kartsa, North Ossetia, Russian Federation, August 13, 1994. At the time, General Savvin was the commander of the Russian Interior Ministry (MVD) Internal Troops (VV).

Violations by Ingush Forces

The Russian human rights group *Memorial* reported that seven Ossetian hostages were killed by Ingush fighters in Kartsa at a club during the fighting.[119]

KURTAT

Kurtat, a largely Ingush village of some four hundred homes, lies about six kilometers northeast of Vladikavkaz, south of Chermen.[120] From its eastern edge, it is about eight kilometers from the Ingush border. Fighting erupted there during the conflict, and both sides took hostages and killed civilians during the "hot" stage of the unrest. But the Ingush eventually were overwhelmed by the numerically-superior, better-armed, and better-organized Ossetian forces. Consequently, all Ingush were expelled from the village, and their homes looted, burned, and often destroyed. Of the 302 Ingush homes, 290 were completely destroyed; of the 102 Ossetian homes, ten were fully destroyed and two partially. No Ingush remain in Kurtat, and the Muslim cemetery, while unharmed, sits untended, choked by weeds and high grass.

Violations by Ossetian Forces

Ahmet, thirty-four, was a native of Kurtat before he was forced out of the village by advancing Ossetian forces in early November 1992.[121] His aunt and uncle were taken hostage and the latter was killed. His body was discovered in early 1993. Ahmet's home was looted and burned.

According to Ahmet, the fighting started on the morning of October 31, when firing from the southwest, from Dachnoye, woke him at 1:00 A.M. Previously, Ossetian Interior Ministry APCs stood outside the village, ostensibly to protect it, but now these same APCs started to fire into the village. Ahmet described the public perception of events at the time to Human Rights Watch:

---

[119] See "Cherez Dva Goda," p. 38.

[120] Human Rights Watch/Helsinki researchers visited Kurtat and toured the village. Almost all Ingush homes had been looted and destroyed.

[121] Human Rights Watch/Helsinki interview, Gaziyurt, Ingushetiya, Russian Federation, August 17, 1994. The displaced from Ingushetiya are housed on the first floor of the village school, while classes are held on the second floor.

> On the second day we began to evacuate the women and the elderly, those who didn't refuse to leave. The first couple of days or so people hoped that they would be helped because it was announced that Russian peacekeeping troops were being dispatched to the conflict zone. I too thought that Russia would stand between the Ingush and the Ossetians and that the situation would return to normal. But people deceived themselves on this. Many of the elderly didn't leave, thinking that soon the troops would come and save them.

But as time went on, the situation grew worse. The village began to be shelled, and houses started to burn. The Ossetians committed their APCs to the battle, and the Ingush fired back with light weapons. Shrapnel from the firing endangered the evacuation, and hit cars and trucks packed with Ingush heading out of the village. Ahmet made several trips with his car along the Chermen road, which came increasingly under fire as the conflict continued. He left Kurtat for the last time on November 4, 1992, when he fled northeast through the field toward the Ingush border.

Many of those unable or unwilling to leave were allegedly killed or taken hostage when Ossetian forces took the village, and Ahmet reports that his aunt and uncle, Huseyin and Malikat Dzharakov, were killed. Huseyin was sixty, Malikat seventy-four years old. Ahmet explains that,

> They didn't leave, but stayed. They had hope....This old woman worked her whole life and just didn't know what could happen. She is still missing, but we buried him [Huseyin] in February 1993. We were brought nine corpses in that month. I immediately recognized him. Every corpse had one ear cut off.

One of Ahmet's neighbors was among the nine corpses, Makkharip Gorbakov, age sixty-five. Ahmet reported that many of the corpses had been mutilated.

Khaziza I., age thirty, lived in the village of Kurtat until forced out during the fighting. In the unrest she reports losing her father, Uvais, age sixty-seven, and her uncle, Magomet. They all lived in the village of Oktyabr'skoye. She explained the events of that fall as follows:

> The situation was very tense the last few days before hostilities broke out. Everything started on the night of October 31. We fled the village on November 5. Houses were burning from the fire and Russian APCs had already started to enter the village.

My own house was burned, and we fled to any house where it was safer. Finally, we were taken away by bus, but many had to flee over the fields. There is nothing left from [the Ingush section of] the village. And our neighbors took all the belongings of our house.

My whole family was taken hostage—mother, father—on October 30 or 31, and held for nine days. Then they released everyone, but for some reason my father was taken away. He was the Mullah. My mother saw him being taken away. No one has heard of him since. My uncle stayed when his family had left and was taken hostage. He hasn't been heard from since.[122]

Violations by Ingush Forces

Ossetians also suffered in Kurtat as a result of the fighting. Although only about ten of the Ossetian homes were destroyed (out of approximately ninety in all), reportedly at least one Ossetian family was robbed and harrassed and one of the family members was allegedly murdered, in contradiction to a statement made by an Ingush from Kurtat who was interviewed by Human Rights Watch:

Although there were one hundred Ossetian households, the Ingush didn't touch one ethnic Ossetian. Moreover, women were not touched. Of course, there were those eager to [harm women].[123]

A retired Ossetian woman lived in Kurtat with her extended family. During the October-November 1992 events she alleges that her house was looted, and her husband, who stayed behind when Ossetian militia men evacuated her and others, was abducted and murdered. She told Human Rights Watch that the phone lines to her house were cut on October 29, and a day later she and her neighbor, who was driving her to work, were stopped at a roadblock manned by armed Ingush, one of whom she recognized as a neighbor. The Ingush there threatened them with rifles and forced the man to move some concrete blocks. According to her, shooting started on the morning of October 31, at around 2:00 A.M. The next

---

[122] Human Rights Watch/Helsinki interview, Gaziyurt, August 17, 1994.

[123] Human Rights Watch//Helsinki interview, Gaziyurt, Ingushetiya, Russian Federation, August 17, 1994.

morning she witnessed buses bringing in armed fighters and leaving with Ingush women and children. These armed Ingush fighters were reportedly not locals, but that day other Ingush fighters, local young men according to her, came to her home, stole two family cars, clothes, and jewelry on the pretext of searching for weapons. She related that,

> That day, a group of young Ingush, high-school students, the oldest was maybe twenty-three, came to our house. They immediately went to our car....He said they were going to trade the car for automatic rifles in Grozny. That day still others came, turned the house upside down, searching for weapons. They took anything they wanted. Suits, women's clothing, gold. They tied everything in a sheet put it in the car [and left]. Later others came and took our other car.[124]

The woman believed her situation and that of her family was hopeless when late on October 31, 1992, two armed Ingush, people she recognized as her neighbors, came and announced: "Get ready, we're going to take you to Nazran, you'll be okay there."

On the morning of November 1, 1992, before sunrise, Ossetian forces on APCs from the direction of Sunzha in the southeast managed to break through to the woman's home.[125] With the Ossetian APCs providing cover, she and her family—but not her sixty-eight-year-old husband—ran through the fields. "We went by foot through the fields, it was raining, the fields had been plowed, everyone was falling." She believes that her husband was taken by Ingush fighters and killed. His body was found one month later. The woman told Human Rights Watch that, "They tortured him as they wanted...we only identified him through his clothes."

---

[124] Human Rights Watch/Helsinki interview, Kurtat, North Ossetia, Russian Federation, August 16, 1994.

[125] Sunzha and Kambilevskoye lie to the southeast of Kurtat. Both are predominately Ossetian villages. Of the 1661 homes in Kambilevskoye, only 197 were Ingush. One hundred ninety-two were destroyed during the conflict or after, while only thirty-seven Ossetian homes were.

VLADIKAVKAZ

Violations by Ossetian Forces

Approximately 17,000 Ingush resided in Vladikavkaz, the North Ossetian capital, and its surrounding areas. Today practically none remain. Of the 171 homes destroyed in Vladikavkaz, 166 belonged to Ingush. In addition, 800 apartments owned by Ingush were seized and their inhabitants forced out.

Mrs. S., thirty-seven years old, lived in Vladikavkaz on Vladikavkaz street in a family dormitory with her husband and nine children, who ranged in age from one to eighteen. She reports that she and her children were taken hostage at 1:00 A.M. on Saturday, October 31, 1992, by North Ossetian OMON forces. She and her family members were taken to Mairamadag, a village west of Vladikavkaz, and held in a basement until exchanged two weeks later. She states that,

> Friday, October 30, was quiet, but on Saturday morning, October 31, I turned on the TV, and the news announced that a war had started. That was in the morning. After lunch, some men dressed in civilian clothes came to the apartment and said, "Go wherever you want, but get out of here." I had never seen these people before.[126]

She called her parents in Kartsa, who told her to stay put because women and children would not be harmed. She took their advice, but later that day North Ossetian OMON troops returned, this time violently. Mrs. S. explains that,

> At about 1:00 A.M. Sunday morning, there was banging on the door. I went up to it, heard male voices, and became frightened and didn't open the door. I stood, my legs shaking, the banging continued, it was horrible. Finally, they bashed the door in and shouted, "What is your nationality." I figured if I said, "Ingush," they would kill me, so I remained quiet. This angered one of them, who fired a pistol. I fell to the floor, wounded.

Carried in a blanket, Mrs. S. and the children were herded off to a waiting bus and then taken to Mairamadag, where they were held in a basement for two

---

[126] Human Rights Watch/Helsinki interview, Gaziyurt, Ingushetiya, Russian Federation, August 17, 1994.

weeks. During that time, according to Mrs. S., both men and women were taken away and beaten and humiliated. She told Human Rights Watch that, "They would take people in the evening and then return them towards morning in such a condition." Finally, Mrs. S. and her children were exchanged and sent to Nazran, where she underwent an operation for her wound.

ZAVODSKII (A SUBURB OF VLADIKAVKAZ)

Violations by Ossetians Forces

Kuresh, age sixty-two, lived in Zavodskii, a mostly Ossetian settlement a few kilometers north of Vladikavkaz. Born in the Prigorodnyi region, he was deported with his family in 1944 to Kazakhstan, returning fifteen years later. On October 31, 1992, on his way to a funeral in Kartsa, he reports that he was taken hostage after boarding a bus near the "Druzhba" movie theater in Vladikavkaz and held nine days before being exchanged. He explains that,

> I got on the number 12 bus at about 3:00 P.M. at the "Druzhba Theater." Then some North Ossetian OMON stopped the bus before we got to the corn market and told me to get on another bus. They didn't hurt me, just asked for my papers, which I didn't have with me. They put me in a cellar that was full of people.[127]

Kuresh was then taken to grain storage facility outside of the village of Gizel, about five kilometers west of Vladikavkaz. "This place was packed. Every minute they brought someone. They even had two Ossetians and a Russian, but they were quickly released."

The next day, he was taken by truck with other hostages to Mairamadag, where three of his family members—also detained by Ossetian forces—joined him. They were held in a basement near a pigsty. Part of the time he was treated well and given food, while part of the time he was not fed. On November 9, 1992, he and his family members were exchanged along with three other busloads of Ingush for Ossetian hostages.

What happened to Kuresh's wife Maryam and his youngest son Murat underscores the largely negative role refugees from South Ossetia played in the conflict. While a North Ossetian neighbor hid them and tried to help them, South

---

[127] Human Rights Watch/Helsinki interview, Refugee camp "Zavodskii," Nazran, Ingushetiya, Russian Federation, August 17, 1994.

Ossetian refugees looted the home and a policeman originally from South Ossetian reportedly torched the remains. Maryam told Human Rights Watch that,

> Two of our neighbors, both Ossetians, hid us. When they took the rest of our men away, our neighbors told Valeri Tsikoyev, the local militiaman to leave me and my daughter-in-law alone, and we remained at home with our youngest child, Murat. Then they hid us for six days.[128]

Maryam, however, did not want to abandon her home, and on the evening of November 5, 1992, she, her daughter-in-law, and son returned home. Later that night she reports that they were taken hostage by a militiaman and fifteen other men, who then proceeded to loot and burn the house. Maryam explained:

> That militiaman, who is originally from South Ossetia, came with fifteen men to take us away. Were we that powerful, two women and a boy, that they needed fifteen men? They didn't let us take anything. These southerners, how many times I gave them things, they were refugees from South Ossetia. They looted all our things. Then the militiaman burned our house down.

Maryam and her son were taken to a medical institute in Vladikavkaz near the movie theater "Druzhba," but her daughter-in-law, who was half-Ossetian and half-Russian, returned to her father's family. The next day Maryam, her son, and thirty-four other Ingush hostages were exchanged for sixteen Ossetian hostages.

TARSKOYE

Violations By Ossetian Forces

Tarskoye, a majority Ossetian village (284 Ingush homes; 529 Ossetian) is located in a valley at the foothills of the Caucasian mountains approximately ten kilometers southeast of Vladikavkaz. Even by the admission of Ossetians with whom we spoke, there was no fighting in the village during the conflict. Despite the lack of fighting, 190 of the Ingush homes were fully destroyed and sixty-one partially damaged. One Ossetian woman in the village told us, "Luckily, all the

---

[128] Human Rights Watch/Helsinki interview, Zavodskii Refugee Camp, Nazran, Ingushetiya, Russian Federation, August 18, 1994.

Ossetian homes were undamaged...I don't know [about the destroyed Ingush homes], maybe they themselves wrecked them. They blame us for everything."[129] An Ossetian militiaman in the village told us that the Ingush had not fought and that all the houses had been destroyed wantonly by the Ossetians as an act of anger.[130]

Ossetian forces also reportedly took hostages and committed murder. Troops from a nearby Russian military base helped to evacuate civilians, but did little to stop the destruction of homes or other violations of humanitarian law.

An elderly Ingush man, Magomet K., had taken refuge at the Russian base, but on November 5, 1992, he returned to his home, already ransacked by Ossetian forces. Shortly thereafter he reports that he was taken hostage by Ossetian paramilitaries. Magomet alleges that three other Ingush hostages who were with him were later found murdered. He recounts that,

> We entered Tarskoye after everyone had left, we were hiding at the Russian base. It must have been November 5 or something. We went to our home, everything was broken and destroyed. When we went out on the street again, an APC from the direction of Yuzhnyi came and stopped us in the street. They asked why we were here and I pointed to my house, but they only said, "Come to our headquarters." There were eight people there. We left there and the Ossetians went into another house and arrested Muzkhmadbashi Temirkhanov, and a women named Tamara, age 22, and Sultan B. I was put in one car, the other three in another vehicle. We didn't see them again, I think they shot them by the road. I was held for ten days in Vladikavkaz, in a stable....Finally they exchanged fifty of us for fifty Ossetians, but when they did the exchange they took away some young people who didn't come back.[131]

Human Rights Watch spoke with the wife of Sultan B. She asserts that they stayed in Tarskoye until November 4th, 1992, and then escaped through the mountains to Ingushetiya with the whole family. Her mother-in-law was ill and

---

[129] Human Rights Watch/Helsinki interview, Tarskoye, August 19, 1994.

[130] Human Rights Watch/Helsinki interview, Tarskoye, August 19, 1994.

[131] Human Rights Watch/Helsinki interview, Gaziyurt, August 17, 1994.

could not continue on, so her husband took her back to the village. A brother-in-law accompanied the two. That was the last day she saw her husband alive. Parts of his body were discovered six months later. According to her,

> On the fifth day it was impossible to stay in the village, so we went into the woods to spend the night...But to get to safety we had to go through the mountains, and many couldn't make it. So I continued with our children and my father-in-law and my husband, Sultan B., returned to the village with his mother, who was quite ill. My brother in-law also returned. They were all taken hostage, but my husband was taken away and killed. They found his remains [and those of two others killed] six months later. They brought little bits of bones. Dogs, wild hogs had eaten the corpses.

OTHER VIOLATIONS IN 1994

Killings and hostage-taking continued sporadically in 1994. April and May were extremely tense months in the state of emergency region:

- On March 30, three Ossetians were taken hostage (Tebiyev, Khamitsayev, and Byazrov);

- On April 7, in Ingushetiya, Ozdoyev was killed and his two friends Aspiyev and Gagiyev were taken hostage;

- On April 12, a column of Ingush headed to Kartsa from Nazran was stopped outside their destination and taken hostage, though they were later freed;

- On May 19, six Ingush, citizens of North Ossetia, were taken hostage on their way to Kartsa. As of this writing, they are still missing;

- In May, eight Georgian road builders were killed working in Ingushetiya at the Assinovskii gorge on the Alkun-Targim road;[132]

- On Sunday, June 12, 1994, two soldiers from the former Temporary Administration, serving in the Special Investigative Group (OSOG) of the MVD, were shot and killed in Malgobek, a town in Ingushetiya. Major Vadim Ivanovich Moiseyev and Sergeant Danil' Khikmatullovich Baidashev were shot seven times. Both men were unarmed.[133]

OFFICIAL RUSSIAN CASUALTY FIGURES[134]

Total dead as of June 31, 1994: 644

Those killed through November 4, 1992:
        Ossetian: 151
        Ingush: 302
        Other Nationalities: 25
        North Ossetian Ministry of the Interior: 9
        Russian Ministry of Defense: 8
        Russian Ministry of the Interior, Internal Troops: 3

---

[132] "Beseda c pervyim Zamestitelem Glavy Vremennoi Administratsii, Generalom Nikolayem Vod'ko," ("Conversation with the First Deputy to the Head of the Temporary Administration, General Nikolai Vod'ko,") *Vestnik Vremennoi Administratsii*, Vladikavkaz, North Ossetia, Russian Federation, June 17, 1994, p. 1. Henceforth, "Beseda."

Vestnik is the paper of the Temporary Administration and is published and written for both the Ingush and Ossetian communities in Ingushetiya and North Ossetia.

[133] "Press-Reliz ot 14 Iyunya 1994, 'Vystrely V Spinu,'Press-Tsentr VA," ("Press Release of June 14, 1994, 'Shots in the Back,' Press-Center Temporary Administration,") *Vestnik Vremennoi Administratsii*, Vladikavkaz, North Ossetia, Russian Federation, June 17, 1994, p. 1.

[134] *Raion Chrezvychainogo Polozheniya (Severnaya Osetiya I Ingushetiya), (The Region of Emergency Rule: North Ossetia and Ingushetiya,)* Vladikavkaz, North Ossetia, 1994, p. 63. This compilation of reports, statistics, and documents is published by the Temporary Administration. Hereafter, *Raion Chrezvychainogo Polozheniya*. These figures differ somewhat from Russian Federation Procuracy figures given earlier in footnote 91.

Those killed between November 5, 1992 and December 31, 1992:
>   Ossetian: 9
>   Ingush: 3
>   Other Nationalities: 2
>   Unknown Nationalities: 12
>   Unified Investigative Group, Ministry of the Interior: 1

Those killed in 1993:
>   Ossetian: 40
>   Ingush: 33
>   Other Nationalities: 21
>   Unknown Nationalities: 30
>   North Ossetian Ministry of the Interior: 9
>   Ingush Ministry of the Interior: 5
>   Russian Ministry of Defense: 3
>   Russian Ministry of the Interior, Internal Troops: 4
>   Unified Investigative Group, Russian Ministry of the Interior: 8

Those killed as of June 31, 1994:
>   Ossetian: 6
>   Ingush: 3
>   Other Nationalities: 7
>   Russian Ministry of Defense: 1
>   Russian Ministry of the Interior, Internal Troops: 2
>   Unified Investigative Group, Russian Ministry of the Interior: 4

VI. RUSSIAN POLICY AND CONDUCT

THE TEMPORARY ADMINISTRATION

The Russian Federal government has ultimate responsibility for the conduct of all state forces, including Russian Defense Ministry and Interior Ministry, North Ossetian Interior Ministry, and Ingush Interior Ministry troops, that operate in the Prigorodnyi region of North Ossetia or in contiguous territories. On November 2, 1992, the Russian government instituted a state of emergency in the Prigorodnyi region and certain areas of North Ossetia and Ingushetiya. The emergency rule decree, which the Russian legislature renewed every two months, remained in force until February 1, 1995. The so-called "Temporary Administration" set up in accord with this decree had complete executive power over the territory covered by the emergency rule decree, including over Ingush and North Ossetian authorities as well as over Russian federal forces. It constituted the state body on the ground responsible for upholding the law and protecting human rights. The head of the Temporary Administration was directly subordinate to the President Boris Yeltsin. The Russian Defense and Interior Ministry forces and the Federal Counter-intelligence Service (FSK) were all operationally subordinated to the head of the Temporary Administration in the area under emergency rule. Article 5 of the emergency rule decree also ordered that, "measures be taken to prevent armed conflict between the opposing sides and for the defense and safety of citizens and for the rigorous enforcement of the emergency rule regime." [135]

On November 4, 1992, after a request by the North Ossetian president, a new presidential decree was issued whereby organs of state power and local self

---

[135] Under the emergency rule decree, the Temporary Administration enjoyed the powers to censor the press, to expel violators of public order, and to suspend activities of political parties and other social groups. It had about 3,000 Russian Interior Ministry troops, who rotated out about every month, under its direct command. Throughout the state of emergency, public meetings, elections, demonstrations, rallies or street marches, and selling weapons were supposed to be banned. For a copy of the emergency rule decree, see, Moscow, ITAR-TASS, Foreign Broadcast Information Service (FBIS), Central Eurasia, February 1, 1995.

rule bodies were allowed to continue to operate in the region.[136] While this new decree created a situation of dual power whereby local authorities would have to obey both their own government edicts and those of the Temporary Administration, it did not diminish the ultimate responsibility of the Russian Federal government through the Temporary Administration for actions of local North Ossetian and Ingush security forces.

In reality, however, the Temporary Administration made little use of any of its authority, hampered by the dual power situation. Demonstrations by both sides were often held. Groups of angry Ossetians gathered to block physically the return of displaced Ingush to their homes. Little was achieved in disarming the population. Radical groups printed and distributed inflammatory literature. On August 1, 1993, gunmen, believed to be Ingush, assassinated the head of the Temporary Administration, Viktor Polyanichko as well as two other officials.[137] Aleksandr Kotenkov, the third head of the Temporary Administration, maintained that elections were illegal under the emergency rule decree but admitted that he had little power to prevent a presidential election in Ingushetiya. He complained that, "By law, elections, demonstrations and meetings are not allowed in the emergency rule zone. But on the other hand, how can I prevent this? Use force? Absurd. Even if we would block off the building where the people meet they would find another place."[138]

On February 7, 1995, the Council of the Federation, the upper house of the Russian parliament, failed to renew the decree in spite of government approval

---

[136] Under this dual power arrangement, local executive powers were supposed to carry out the laws and orders of the republic's executive authorities and local self-administration while at the same time following the edicts and instructions of the Temporary Administration. It was not until November 30, 1993 that another presidential decree returned sole power over organs of state power in the emergency rule zone to the Temporary Administration, including the right to fire civil servants. In April 1994, another presidential decree gave the Temporary Administration the right to stop the actions of decrees issued by local government executive bodies if they contradicted Temporary Administration orders, laws of the Russian federation, or presidential decrees. See "Cherez Dva Goda," pp. 66-7.

[137] "Gunmen on Horses Slay 3 in Ossetian Region," *Washington Post*, August 3, 1993.

[138] A. Yevtushenko, "Kavkaz so strakhom zhdet vesny," *Komsomol'skaya Pravda* (Moscow), January 23, 1993, p. 1.

of the measure, and the state of emergency was revoked.[139] In its place the Russian government under Presidential Decree #139 created a Temporary State Committee ("Vremennyi Gosudarstvennii Komitet") on the basis of the Temporary Administration.

While the new Temporary State Committee is considered the legal successor of the Temporary Administration, it has diminished powers and is not the overall executive power in the area as was its predecessor.[140] However, the Russian Federal government still has ultimate responsibility for the actions of all state actors in the region.

CULPABILITY OF THE RUSSIAN GOVERNMENT

Determining those responsible for the outbreak of hostilities would require a large-scale investigation and access to classified Russian and Ossetian government documents—both of which are beyond the scope of this report. However, it seems clear from available evidence that once fighting broke out, the Russian government failed in its obligations to protect human life and property in the Prigorodnyi region of North Ossetia in spite of public claims that it had control over the situation.

From the first day of the conflict, high-level Russian security personnel and other government officials were on the ground in both North Ossetia and Ingushetiya. Within a week of the conflict, Russian Defense Minister Pavel Grachev toured the scene of fighting. In spite of this intense and direct involvement, serious mistakes were made. Russian officials disbursed large numbers of weapons to North Ossetian authorities, who then handed them out to both North Ossetian security officers and to paramilitary groups and militias. Russian forces did not separate opposing Ingush fighters and North Ossetian security forces and paramilitaries, thus allowing the civilian population to remain where they were. Such an intervention, conducted early in the conflict, might have prevented the forced migration of the vast majority of Ingush living in the

---

[139] "Ukaz o ChP otmenen," ("Decree on the State of Emergency,") *Rossiskaya Gazeta* (Moscow), February 22, 1995, p. 11. In October 1994 the Council of Federation also initially refused to approve the emergency rule decree for the Prigorodnyi region.

[140] The Temporary State Committee was given the task of coordinating the activities of federal executive bodies as well as those of Ingushetiya and North Ossetia in overcoming the crisis in the region connected with the conflict.

Prigorodnyi region. Rather, Russian forces either aided in the evacuation of Ingush civilians—"polite" forced evacuation—or spearheaded attacks against villages held by Ingush militants, forcing out both civilians and fighters. While in some cases such evacuations saved lives, the end result was the same: eviction of the Ingush population. Russian forces either could not or refused to stop the wanton destruction and looting of Ingush homes and property, which continued long after the "hot" stage of the conflict ended on November 5. Although Russian forces had ostensibly established some control over the Prigorodnyi region under an emergency rule decree, they allowed North Ossetian paramilitaries and others to loot systematically and destroy large numbers of Ingush homes and property. Indeed, most Ingush dwellings were destroyed after November 5, 1992.

From the first day of the conflict, high-level Russian government officials were on the scene of fighting and stated that the situation was under control. On October 31, 1992, a high-level Russian delegation arrived in Vladikavkaz including Deputy Prime Minister Georgii Khizha, Chairman of the State Committee for Emergency Situations S.K. Shoigu and his assistant Col. General Filatov, and the commander of Russian Interior Ministry Internal Troops Col. General Savvin. They approved the disbursement of hundreds of light weapons to Ossetian MVD troops, which also found their way into the hands of Ossetian paramilitaries. On November 1, 1992, Itar-Tass reported that two regiments of Russian paratroopers were sent to the conflict region to support MVD troops.[141] On November 2, a state of emergency was declared in the paramilitary Prigorodnyi region, and Deputy Prime Minister Khizha was named head of the "Temporary Administration," charged with the task of ending the conflict. In a telephone interview with the Moscow daily *Izvestiya*, on the evening of November 3, 1992, Khizha stated that he had at his disposal sufficient forces to separate the fighters, and that a majority of the villages were under his control, thanks to the decisive action by Russian paratroopers, MVD units, and Ossetian paramilitaries.[142]

During talks held on November 4, 1992, between Khizha and Issa Kostoyev, President Yeltsin's representative in Ingushetiya, a cease-fire was

---

[141] "Russia Sends More Troops to the Caucasus," *The New York Times*, November 2, 1992.

[142] "Chrezvychainoye Polozheniye v Severnoi Osetii deistvuyet. No Krovoprolitiye prodolzhayetsya" ("The State of Emergency in North Ossetia is in Force. The Blood-letting Continues,") *Izvestiya* (Moscow), November 5, 1992, p. 1.

As of November 3, 1992, Russian casualties were reported as three dead, and six wounded. All were paratroopers.

announced and supposed to take effect at 8:00 P.M. that day. The cease-fire envisioned Russian military occupation of all villages in the Prigorodnyi region, disbanding of all armed bands, free passage for refugees, and exchange of prisoners and hostages. According to reports from the scene, by 6:00 P.M., November 4, 1992, Kurtat and Dachnoye were taken back by OMON, republican guard, and paramilitaries of North Ossetia. At that time all populated areas previously held by Ingush fighters were under the control of Russian forces, MVD troops of North Ossetia, North Ossetia Republican guards, or militia forces.[143] By this time almost all Ingush resistance had been broken, though isolated shots were heard throughout the area.

Within a week after fighting broke out, Defense Minister Pavel Grachev personally became involved in managing the crisis. On November 5, 1992, Grachev—accompanied by Security Minister Victor Barannikov—flew to Vladikavkaz to oversee Russian military operations. Grachev gave the first hint that official statements were inaccurate:

> I came here with the Ministers of Security and the Interior of the Russian Federation with a clear goal. First, *to ascertain for myself what the situation is, since reports from different sources are, to say the least, not the same and at times contradict each other*; second, to look into the activities of Russian units, including those of Internal Ministry troops: what tasks they have been given, how are they carrying them out, what are the results....finally,...to jointly pass a resolution dealing with the cordoning off and disarming of nationalist bands of both sides."[144]

Resignations and reassignments in ministries involved in stabilizing the Prigorodnyi conflict were the first indications of a botched operation. Georgii Khizha barely served one week as head of the former Temporary Administration when he was replaced by Sergei Shakhrai on November 9, 1992. Four days earlier Shakrai was appointed the head of the State Committee on Nationalities

---

[143] Natal'ya Pachegina and Igor' Terekhov, "Boi v Prigorodnom Raione Prekratilis,'" ("Fighting in the Prigorodnyi Region has Stopped,"), *Nezavisimaya Gazeta* (Moscow), November 6, 1992, p. 1.

[144] Vasilii Fatygarov, "My Vypolnim Ukaz Prezidenta Rossii'" ("We will Carry Out the President's Decree,") *Krasnaya Zvezda* (Moscow), November 7, 1992, p. 1. Italics added.

(*Goskomnats*) with the rank of Deputy Prime Minister.[145] In mid-November 1992, Lieutenant General Vasilii Savvin, the commander of Internal Forces of the Russian MVD, resigned without official explanation shortly after returning from North Ossetia.[146]

Some early press reports alleged problems because of the supposed Russian forces' pro-Ossetian stance. One paper reported how Yuri N., a lieutenant in the Russian military, deserted rather than fight against the civilian population. He explained that,

> I decided it was better to desert than to take part in this. What I saw was horrible. Armed Ossetian units followed right behind us into these villages, annihilating and robbing the peaceful inhabitants, the Ingush. We did not have the right to intervene—no orders. In my opinion a regiment of Russian troops sent into the region was intentionally held up at the airport in Vladikavkaz so that the Ossetians could operate without any hindrance. I know that several of my fellow officers also intend to desert so as not to besmirch themselves for the rest of their lives.[147]

Others also accused Russian forces of failing to prevent civilian deaths and destruction. In late November 1992, only three weeks after the height of the fighting, a group of leading liberals such as Yelena Bonner and Yuri Afanas'yev published a letter criticizing Georgi Khizha, and his deputy, General Filatov. They wrote:

> President Yeltsin's decree instituting a state of emergency in the two republics [Ingushetiya and North Ossetia] was necessary. But at the beginning it was the conduct of those who had been ordered to carry out the decree, i.e. above all Deputy Prime

---

[145] Vasilii Kononenko, "Shakhrai Otpravlyayut vo Vladikavkaz, chtoby sokhranit' balans sil v Pravitel'stve" ("Shakhrai is Being Sent to Vladikavkaz to Keep the Balance of Forces in the Government"), *Izvesitya* (Moscow), November 11, 1992, p. 2.

[146] Vadim Belykh, "General Savvin podal raport i ushel v otpusk ("General Savin Gave his Resignation and Went on Vacation,") *Izvestiya* (Moscow), November 12, 1992, p. 2.

[147] "Armiya v ochage Konflikta," ("Army in the Heart of the Conflict"), *Rossiiskiye Vesti*, (Moscow), November 12, 1992, p. 1.

Minister Khizha as well as General Filatov and others, that led to even more tragic consequences. These people flouted the president's decree and must answer for it in the most serious of terms.[148]

An unpublished official report prepared by the Unified Investigative-Operational Group of the Procuracy of the Russian Federation, the Russian Ministry of Security, and the Russian Ministry of Internal Affairs harshly criticized the inaction of security forces, their failure to prevent harm to civilians, and their pro-Ossetian conduct.[149] The document, "A Political Evaluation [Draft] by the Security Council of the Russian Federation on the circumstances of the armed conflict on the territory of the North Ossetian SSR and the Ingush Republic in October-November 1992," states that,

> In the first few days of halting the conflict internal troops of the Ministry of the Interior were idle (*bezdeistvoval*), which armed formations from North Ossetia and units of volunteers from South Ossetia used to "free" the settlements of Kartsa and the villages of Terk and Chernorechenskoye....According to the conclusion of the [leadership] of the Unified Investigative-Operational Group of of the Procuracy of the Russian Federation, the Ministry of Security, and the Ministry of Internal Affairs, in the first days of the conflict, the character and the means of bringing into action emergency rule did not fulfill the goals and tasks for which it was introduced. In the emergency rule region armed groups, including those from South Ossetia, continued to operate. Unified forces from the Ministry of the Interior and the Defense Ministry did not separate the hostile sides, did not liquidate or localize armed formations, did not disarm them....The prompt introduction of forces could have prevented such a number of casualties among the civilian population. In a number of cases with the direct connivance of

---

[148] Yu Afanas'yev, L. Batkin, Ye. Bonner, Yu. Burtin, Yu. Morits, M. Pavlova-Sil'vanskaya, L. Timofeyev, "Severnaya Osetiya—Ingushetiya: Put' K Miru Lezhit Cherez Moskvu," ("North Ossetia—Ingushetiya: The Path to Peace Lies through Moscow," *Izvesitya* (Moscow), November 27, 1992, p. 3.

[149] "Draft Political Evaluation," *Nezavisimaya Gazeta*, March 23, 1994, p. 5.

armed forces of the Russian Ministry of the Interior and the North Ossetian Interior Ministry armed formations of the hostile sides committed violence against civilians, robbed, looted, torched and blew up houses, illegally settled in houses abandoned by their inhabitants.[150]

The village of Kartsa, a suburb of Vladikavkaz, presents a clear example of how Russian forces helped evacuate Ingush but then did little to prevent Ossetian paramilitaries from wantonly destroying civilian homes and looting. In Chermen and other villages, Russian forces spearheaded attacks on villages held by Ingush militants, but then allowed North Ossetian security forces and paramilitaries to enter and wreak havoc. One Ingush displaced from Chermen declared to Human Rights Watch that, "The Russians went forward, and after them the Ossetians."[151]

Zekram Musiyev, a local community leader of about one thousand Ingush who returned to Kartsa, complained about the duality of Russian policy. While the military commander at *Sputnik* helped people escape and gave them refuge, Russian forces seemed to do little to prevent wide-scale looting and destruction of Kartsa by Ossetian forces once the fighting was over. According to Mr. Musiyev,

> His name was Boshko, the commander of the division [at Sputnik]. He was then a colonel, he has since become a General. He told us then, "I'm simply a military man—We are the army. We're not the Ministry of the Interior, and therefore we're not allowed to leave the base and help you. We don't have such orders. But if you reach the base, we have every right to protect you." And that's why people fled there. He really helped us in this. And people are grateful to him. We are grateful to him—I would even say—for his courage, empathy, and aid—hundreds of people are alive [because of this].[152]

---

[150] Ibid.

[151] Human Rights Watch/Helsinki interview, Maiskii, North Ossetia, August 16, 1994.

[152] It also appears that Russian forces also helped some Ingush civilians evacuate the village itself.

But Musiyev harshly criticizes the Russian forces for the ensuing destruction and looting of the village by Ossetian militias between roughly November 4, 1992, and November 20, 1992. He believes that Russian inaction, complacence, or collusion was responsible for the destruction of one quarter of Kartsa's houses, mostly by burning. Most of the other homes were looted. Musiyev continued that:

> At this time only about ten homes had been torched. I mean up until November 4 [1992]. Then Russian forces arrived and supposedly the Ossetians left, although they came at night and continued to burn homes. On the night of November 16, 1992, forty-eight homes were burned. This is only in one night....And take all the other settlements, and villages when the Ingush fled, they were all more or less in one piece. [Only after this] they started to loot. Looters came, cleaned out houses, took everything away, torched the homes, and left. This continues to this day.

A liberal North Ossetian professor and civic leader believes that the main fault for the outbreak of the conflict lies with Ingush extreme nationalists, but concedes that Russian pro-Ossetian behavior and inaction by Russian authorities before, during, and after the armed clashes exacerbated the conflict.

> The main guilt belongs to the Ingush extremists that pushed their people to this. But we also believe that our local Ossetian authorities and the central powers in Moscow hold a great deal of responsibility. They didn't take adequate measures, although the situation was clear enough and everyone saw where things were headed. When the conflict started, the authorities took a waiting position and there was a belief that Dudayev would enter the conflict. When General Filatov came to Vladikavkaz airport, he directly gave a statement that the Ossetians are our brothers and that we would not let them down. In my opinion that was done especially to get Dudayev into the conflict as an ally of the Ingush, in order to have a reason to invade Chechnya....
>
> The Interior ministry troops should not have waited, but rather should have attempted something to stop both sides, to separate the warring parties. Unfortunately, this was not done. And when it [the conflict] started, they gave people weapons and showed

on TV the killing and the fighting. This elicited a certain response from the population....From the very beginning Russian forces should have taken a much clearer position, both on a political and a tactical level. Those homes that were destroyed, the majority of them were laid waste to not during the fighting, but after. And the authorities looked the other way. There was a kind of euphoria. We were the victors. And where were the Russian authorities?

On the third day the Russian Army came in tanks. There were homes destroyed during military operations, but most of them were destroyed after the war by our side. Everyone saw what had happened. And because of this there was hatred, and people started to destroy homes. But the authorities should have kept cool heads and put a stop to this....maybe it was impossible to stop this. Everyone was so angry.[153]

In the village of Tarskoye, Russian forces "evacuated" Ingush who lived there, but then, as in Kartsa, did little to stop Ossetian paramilitaries from destroying their homes, despite the presence of a nearby Russian army base.

An Ossetian militia soldier from Tarskoye openly told Human Rights Watch that all the destruction in the village came after the Ingush had fled and was intentional, not the result of fighting. In fact, there had not even been a battle in the town between the sides:

There was no shoot-out in Tarskoye...[The Ingush homes] were fully destroyed after the Ingush left. They left on November 3 or 4, I really don't remember exactly which day. They went through the forest and mountains to Ingushetiya. People were outraged [at the Ingush].[154]

An elderly Ingush man who had lived there told us,

I lived in Tarskoye....and as things turned out, we did not expect what would be. We didn't have any arms at all. The unexpected

---

[153] Human Rights Watch/Helsinki interview with Dzarasov.

[154] Human Rights Watch/Helsinki interview, Tarskoye, North Ossetia, August 19, 1994.

> thundered down on us. I was the last to leave. On October 30 Russian forces took us out of the village. They helped us. Major Molchanov told us, "Comrades, you have to leave." And so we left. He said that he couldn't protect us. And later we heard that Russia was against us. And you can't do anything against Russia.[155]

Tamara, a thirty-year-old Ossetian women, agreed that there had not been fighting in the village, but conjectured that possibly the Ingush themselves had destroyed their own homes:

> On the evening of October 31 firing from all sides could be heard. Our Ingush neighbors did not fire, however, they all fled. They knew that in Oktyabr'skoye and other areas they were unsuccessful, and they ran away like cowards. They were still here on the 30th, but then on the 31st and 1st they started to slip away. We were evacuated on November 1 in buses with armed escorts, and when we returned there were no more Ingush.[156]

Prejudicial Russian behavior during the conflict engendered a deep mistrust of Russian authority among the Ingush population. An Ingush man forcibly displaced from Kurtat commented that:

> Initially people hoped that they would be helped when it was announced that Russian peacekeeping forces were being deployed in the conflict zone. I thought the same thing, that Russian forces would intervene between the Ingush and Ossetians and all would normalize. But people were tricked on this account. And many old people did not leave because of this. They thought, 'well the troops will come and we will be saved.'[157]

---

[155] Human Rights Watch/Helsinki interview, Gaziyurt, Ingushetiya, August 19, 1994.

[156] Human Rights Watch Interview, Tarskoye, North Ossetia, August 19, 1994.

[157] Human Rights Watch/Helsinki interview, Gaziyurt, Ingushetiya, August 17, 1994.

VII. CONCLUSION OF THE CONFLICT

ACCOUNTABILITY AND JUSTICE IN THE PRIGORODNYI CONFLICT

A major obstacle to the long-term reconciliation between Ingush and Ossetians in the Prigorodnyi region derives from the absence of what is referred to in Russian as a "legal judgement" (pravovaya otsenka) of the conflict.[158] Such an judgement would include determining which parties are responsible for the outbreak of the fighting and, more important, bringing to justice those who committed crimes in the conflict. Numerous factors have prevented Russian authorities from producing a legal judgement: failure to make arrests because of stiff opposition from the local authorities and populace; public pressure on investigators and prosecutors; and lack of individuals willing to testify. Ossetians and Ingush alike angrily lament the lack of a legal judgement. One Ossetian official told us that,

> If we were to pass a decree that would simply allow all the Ingush back, the people would simply sweep us out of power....The deputies [of the North Ossetian Supreme Soviet] went to these demonstrations and were told the following: "For the time being we don't want them [the Ingush] to return." Until we know who the killers are....If we are not assured [that an individual did not participate in crimes] when he is returned, we are placing him at risk for vigilante justice, and we will not solve the problem in the zone of conflict that way. You need here a lawful determination of the guilty, you need to separate the wheat from the chaff....There should be conditions from Russia for bringing an end to the conflict, from the central authorities in Moscow. They should provide an analysis of the events, a legal analysis, so that we know who is guilty and who is innocent. I don't mean that a whole people would be guilty, but exactly what concrete individuals are responsible for committing crimes.[159]

---

[158] Human Rights Watch/Helsinki is not concerned with who started the conflict, but merely that those who committed criminal acts be brought to justice.

[159] Human Rights Watch/Helsinki interview with Tsoriyev.

In addition, even in the absence of a judgement, little has been achieved in bringing to justice those who committed individual crimes during and after the fighting. While both sides curse the absence of accountability and justice, they also impede investigations. In addition, both sides often speak as if a "legal judgement" would by definition find the opposing side guilty.

After the events of October/November 1992, investigative groups from the Russian Ministries of Internal Affairs and Security and the Procuracy began operating in the area.[160] On December 16, 1992, the efforts of these three groups were united in the "Unified Investigative-Operative Group (OSOG)," but their new organization only began serious work in February 1993. Its main goal was to investigate the causes and circumstances of the unrest and to identify those who committed crimes.

The work of the OSOG never really got off the ground. Some investigators were sent back to Moscow, some removed from the case, and one was given the task of investigating the events surrounding the rebellion of the Russian Parliament in October 1993. This neglect is reflected in the results of the investigations of OSOG. According to a Russian Foreign Ministry official, 1,600 individuals participated in criminal acts connected with the conflict in 1992; i.e., there are 1,600 individuals against whom sufficient evidence exists to be able to charge them with a crime.[161] Only thirteen cases involving fifteen people, however, have been brought to court, resulting in convictions leading to imprisonment in ten cases. The strictest sentence was seven years, not terribly severe by Russian standards. There were also reports of procedural irregularities in other cases. Recently it was reported that results of investigations by the Russian Procuracy into abuses, while ready, would not be made public.[162]

Both local authorities and the local population impede the work of investigators. The head of the Caucasian Inter-Regional Procuracy, which was formed in June 1994 to coordinate the activities of the Ingush and Ossetian Procuracies and OSOG, complained that,

---

[160] Information in this section from "Cherez Dva Goda", pp. 63-66, unless otherwise cited.

[161] Human Rights Watch/Helsinki interview with Mikhail Alesksandrovich Lebedev, deputy head of the Department on Human Rights, Directory of International Humanitarian and Cultural Cooperation, Ministry of Foreign Affairs, Moscow, August 10, 1994.

[162] Pliyev, *Nezavisimaya Gazeta*, October 27, 1995, p. 3.

> The united investigative groups experience serious pressure and impediments both from the authorities of both republics as well as from their population. I don't completely understand the position of the populace. On the one hand they accuse us of not bringing to justice those who have committed serious crimes, [but] on the other hand I can name a dozen or more of our attempts to detain or arrest [someone] or to conduct a search or some investigative work when we were shown the fiercest opposition. It even occurred that hundreds, thousands of people surrounded an investigative team, which could have resulted in a shoot-out or God knows what. This did not occur thanks to the cool-headedness and wisdom of the leaders of the [investigative] team, who ceased their investigations in order not to provoke a bigger outburst....This active opposition plus a mass of passive resistance, [for example] when people don't show up for questioning or when they show up but don't tell what they witnessed, to a great degree impedes our work. This commenced from the very beginning of our work.

In November 1995 it was announced that the Caucasian Inter-Regional Procuracy was being renamed the Procuracy in the North Caucasus and was being moved from Vladikavkaz to Grozny.[163]

The unpublished Russian government report cited above on the conflict also criticizes legal inaction by Russian authorities. It states that,

> ...[D]ecisions to detain and arrest people are systematically not carried out. This is brought about by the fact that refugees are spread throughout the territory of Ingushetiya and there is not a list of their place of residence. [Also], local law enforcement authorities do not provide assistance in searches. They have not carried one assignment pertaining to this.
>
> On the territory of the North Ossetian ASSR, where in general the population has remained in its place of residency, investigative work is blocked by the local population and illegal

---

[163] Natal'ya Gorodetskaya, "Vladimir Lozovoi opasayetsya obostreniya situatsiya v Severnoi Osetii," ("Vladimir Lozovoi fears an increase in tensions in the situation in North Ossetia,") *Segodnya* (Moscow), February 7, 1996, p. 2.

armed groups. In order to free those detained, hostages are taken, investigative groups are blocked, and mass communal actions are carried out with demands to free those arrested.[164]

The former Temporary Administration complained that its work was hindered by the absence of a "legal judgement." Vladimir Lozovoi, a former head of this government body and now chair of the Temporary State Committee, its successor, told Human Rights Watch that,

> The General Prosecutor of Russia Stepankov committed a grave error, which only at the beginning of this year [1994] has started to be rectified... a legal judgement of the unrest should have been worked out. On the basis of this, one could have brought to justice the individuals who inspired and organized this conflict....Our work suffers from this now.[165]

Mr. Lozovoi's deputy, General Nikolai Vod'ko, avowed that the lack of effective accountability further prevented the restoration of social stability in the region. He told Human Rights Watch, "Undoubtedly these crimes are worsened by the fact that they remain unpunished, which has a negative effect on our operational situation, disturbs public opinion, and evinces mutual recriminations both in the press and in the mass media."[166]

Ossetian and Ingush whom Human Rights Watch interviewed stated that they often personally knew their abuser. An Ossetian woman from Chermen whose husband was killed in 1992 complained angrily about the ineffectiveness of the former Temporary Administration's efforts to bring the guilty to justice. Her example illustrates the effects of the lack of accountability described by Gerneral Vod'ko:

> It's impossible to describe it all. What didn't the Ingush have? And right now none of them are put in prison, and they did such things. That's why we are angry and nervous, if only they punished one criminal we pointed out, in order that people calm

---

[164] "Draft Political Evaluation," *Nezavisimaya Gazeta*, p. 5.

[165] Human Rights Watch/Helsinki interview with Lozovoi, August 16, 1994.

[166] "Beseda", p. 1.

> down. They come [the investigative group], they take information, they leave. Then the next group comes. I must have been questioned about twenty times.[167]

An Ingush man whose relative had been murdered in 1993 shares the same grievance: "They don't do anything....Not one case has been solved. Not one person has been arrested. Already ten investigators have come here....we told them everything."[168]

Another Ossetian woman from Chermen who stated that she had been taken hostage by Ingush militants was able to name four Ingush she personally knew and whom she alleges took an active part in violations against Ossetians. One of these individuals currently lives in her village, albeit in the northern, Ingush end of the settlement. She told us that, "Magomet Ch. and his wife and sister [my neighbors] were standing on the street and pointing [to the Ingush militants], saying, "That's an Ingush home, that's an Ossetian, so is that one."[169] Another Ossetian man from Chermen whose home was destroyed by Ingush militants during the conflict and who had neighbors and relatives killed and taken hostage complained that,

> Everyday the Temporary Administration says that we have to let the Ingush back into the village. How can we let them in when they killed so many relatives? Now they want to live next to me. No one would agree to that....Two years the investigation [into the events of 1992] has been continuing. And the Ingush who come here and want to return say that they have lost their documents. It is impossible to live with the Ingush.[170]

Ingush also knew their attackers and make the same charges. A thirty-seven-year-old Ingush woman taken hostage with her family in Vladikavkaz by

---

[167] Human Rights Watch/Helsinki interview, Chermen, North Ossetia, August 15, 1995.

[168] Human Rights Watch/Helsinki interview, village of Maiskii, North Ossetia, August 14, 1994.

[169] Human Rights Watch/Helsinki interview, Chermen, North Ossetia, August 15, 1995.

[170] Human Rights Watch/Helsinki interview, village of Chermen, North Ossetia, Russian Federation, August 14, 1994.

North Ossetian OMON forces claimed that her neighbors began looting her home even before she had been taken away. "We still hadn't left our home," she told Human Rights Watch that,

> When our neighbors started to grab our possessions. One of them was called Ira K. When they were taking me away I shouted to her, 'Please take some clothes for the children and bring them down,' but she only replied, 'You won't be needing them.'"[171]

An Ingush woman from Zavodskii reported that she knew the individual who burned down her house, a policeman who earlier had a quarrel with her son: "Valerii Ts., a policeman, burned our house down. He had had a fight with my son before the war broke out. Another neighbor, he was a friend of my son, stole our television and some clothing.[172]

The wife of one of the six Ingush hostages from Kartsa seized on May 19, 1994, expressed dismay at the inability of the Temporary Administration either to guarantee the safety of her husband—who at the time was travelling with a Russian officer—or to find and free him.

> I wrote to Lozovoi, I wrote to Galazov...not a word, not a peep, nothing. I wrote to Moscow, I wrote to Yeltsin, I wrote to Chernomyrdin. You see how I live. I spent 65,000 on a telegram to Moscow. Again, nothing, not a word. If Russia doesn't need us, it would have been easier if they let them kill us right on the spot....They took them hostage. Four cars...They really can't figure out who did it? They really can't find them? How is one to understand this?

---

[171] Human Rights Watch/Helsinki interview, Gaziyurt, Ingushetiya, Russian Federation, August 17, 1994.

[172] Human Rights Watch/Helsinki interview, Refugee camp "Zavodskii", Nazran, Ingushetiya, Russian Federation, August 17, 1994.

RECONCILIATION AND THE RETURN OF THE DISPLACED

The reconciliation process between Ingush and Ossetians in the Prigorodnyi region and the return of Ingush displaced to their homes [and the reconstruction of those dwellings] is proceeding slowly, if at all. The war in Chechnya has drawn Russian government attention and resources away from the conflict. The vast majority of the estimated 34,000-64,000 Ingush displaced have not returned to their former homes in Prigorodnyi, and mistrust, tension, and mutual recrimination are as high as at any time since the outbreak of the conflict.[173]

Negotiations and Decrees

In the spring of 1993, negotiations among North Ossetian, Ingush, and Russian officials concerning the 1992 Ingush-Ossetian conflict began. Until late summer 1994, however, the results of these initiatives remained on paper, with few concrete accomplishments. On March 20, 1993, the North Ossetian leader Akhsarbek Galazov and his Ingush counterpart Ruslan Aushev signed the Kislovodsk agreement, named after the North Caucasian resort town where the negotiations were held. The agreement called for the "complex solving of the refugee problem, including questions of security, methods of return, and settlement..."[174] The Kislovodsk agreement stipulated that only those who possessed a valid residency permit in the Prigorodnyi region as of October 31, 1992, and who did not take part in the conflict would be allowed to return. The

---

[173] According to Vladimir Lozovoi, head of the former Temporary Administration and Russian Deputy Prime Minister, there were 46,000 officially registered Ingush displaced as of August 1994. This number is based on figures of the Federal Migration Service. The Ingush Migration Service quotes a figure of 64,000 displaced, while the North Ossetian Passport Service claims that 34,000 Ingush lived in Prigorodnyi in 1992. The discrepancy comes from the fact that many Ingush were not officially registered to live in Prigorodnyi, i.e. they did not possess residency permits, a so-called "propiska." In Ossetia there are 43,000 officially registered Ossetian refugees and displaced. The overwhelming majority of them come from South Ossetia and Georgia, not from Ingushetiya.

Ingush, however, never left the village of Maiskii, though about eighteen Ossetian families fled. In addition, roughly 1,500 Ingush live in Kartsa and maybe another 2,500 in Chermen. They informally began to trickle back to those two settlements after fighting ended in November 1992.

[174] *Raion Chrezvychainogo Polozheniya*, pp. 4-5.

parties also appealed to the former Temporary Administration for financial assistance.

On December 13, 1993, President Yeltsin issued Decree #2131 ordering the return of Ingush displaced initially to four villages in the Prigorodnyi raion (Chermen, Kurtat, Dongaron and Dachnoye). The decree also recognized the Prigorodnyi region as part of North Ossetia. Little was done to carry out this decree until mid-summer 1994 because of a lack of will on the part of central authorities and mutual hostilities by the Ingush and Ossetian governments. On June 26, 1994, under the mediation of Temporary Administration Chief Vladimir Lozovoi, Ingush President Ruslan Aushev and the North Ossetian leader President Akhsarbek Galazov signed an agreement at Beslan, North Ossetia, on the return of Ingush displaced in coordination with President Yeltsin's Decrees #2131 of December 13, 1993, Emergency Rule Decree #1112 of May 30, 1994, and with the Kislovodsk agreement. Decree #2131 had envisioned the return of Ingush to Chermen, Dachnoye, Kurtat, and Dongaron in the Prigorodnyi region but had not been enacted. The Beslan agreement divided the return into two stages: a preliminary stage, whereby security would be established in the region, lists of returnees would be compiled, and infrastructure and schools would be restored; and a second stage during which displaced would be returned to homes that had not been destroyed, temporary housing would be provided to those returning to destroyed homes, reconstruction estimates would be determined, and home owners would be allowed to participate in reconstructing their homes.[175]

Number of Repatriated Ingush

According to the former Temporary Administration, as of February 1, 1995, 571 families (largely Ingush) were approved by the administration and a North Ossetian government commission to return to the four villages mentioned in the December 1993 decree. However, this represents only about one fourth of the

---

[175] *Raion Chrezvychainogo Polozheniyza*, pp. 16-18.

In late August 1994, a meeting was held at the Royal Institute for Peace in Oslo, Norway , between Ingush and Ossetians. The meeting was attended by Aleksandr Dzasokhov, an Ossetian and then Deputy Chairman of the Inter-Parliamentary Committee of the Duma,a nd Isa Kostoyev, an Ingush and a member of the Council of Federation. The Ingush spoke of renouncing all claims to the eastern side of Vladikavkaz, while the Ossetians suggested not hindering Ingush return to the Prigorodnyi region. Nothing came of this meeting. Information on meeting from Dr. John Collarusso, Department of Anthropology, McMaster University.

Conclusion of the Conflict

2,234 Ingush families who had applied to return.[176] Under Decree #2131, a total of 215 families had returned to the four villages from August 1, 1994 to December 15, 1994.[177] In January 1995, an additional twelve Ingush farmilies returned to Dachnoye, one to Kurtat, and five to Kartsa.[178] In March, ninety-nine, in April, seventy, in May, sixteen, and in June, forty families—largely Ingush—returned to the Prigorodnyi region, making a total of 460 mostly Ingush families that had returned to their homes in the region by June 31, 1995.[179] However, the total number of eligible families also increased to 4,349.[180] In August, talks were held among Ingush, North Ossetian, and Russian officials to increase the scope of the Ingush return to include the villages of Kambilevskoye, Tarskoye, Kartsa, and Oktyabrskoye.[181]

At the time of Human Rights Watch visit in August 1994, Ingush officials complained bitterly about the slow pace of return: "Three decrees have been passed on the return of refugees, but not one of them has been carried out. Right now, with the greatest difficulty, resettlement is going on. As of today fifteen families have returned...If this tempo continues, it will take years."[182] While some progress has been made, it falls far short not only of Ingush demands but also of Russian government expectations. According to an August 8, 1994, plan, by September 15, 1994, some 937 Ingush families should have returned to the four villages.[183] A

---

[176] "Tem, Komu Predstoit Vernut'sya," ("Those who will return"), *Vestnik* (Vladikavkaz, North Ossetia) February 10, 1995, p. 1. A total of 2,764 families had valid residency permits according to the 1989 census.

[177] "Spravka" ("Info-Bulletin"), *Vestnik* (Vladikavkav), December 30, 1995.

[178] *Vestnik* (Vladikavkaz), February 15, 1995.

[179] Natal'ya Gorodetskaya, "Prezidenty Severnoi Osetii I Ingushetii nachinayut Peregovory" ("The Presidents of North Ossetia and Ingushetiya Begin Talks"), *Segodnya* (Moscow), July 8, 1995.

[180] Ibid.

[181] Moscow INTERFAX, Foreign Broadcast Information Service (FBIS), Central Eurasia, August 10, 1995, p. 28.

[182] Human Rights Watch/Helsinki interview with Pliyev.

[183] "Cherez Dva Goda," p. 9.

year later the situation had little improved, and Ingush complaints continued: Azamat Nalgiyev, Deputy Speaker of the Ingush Parliament, complained that, "The Ossetian side is still hindering the return of citizens of Ingush nationality who were deported from Prigorodnyi district and the town of Vladikavkaz."[184]

Obstacles to Return

Five obstacles hinder the implementation of the Beslan Agreement and the speedy return of refugees. As mentioned above, talks on ending the crisis have proceeded slowly in spite of Russian presidential decrees intended to speed the process along. Only in June 1994, almost two years after the fighting ended, did both sides agree upon a meaningful document on the return of displaced Ingush to Prigorodnyi. Second, since the conflict was local, many victims on both sides know those who assaulted them, and the continuing lack of accountability has allowed bloodfeuds to replace court-room proceedings. Since the local and federal authorities have failed to bring to justice those guilty of crimes, trust has not been restored. Also, North Ossetians believe that the conflict represents Ingush aggression against their republic. According to the Ossetian perception, the return of Ingush—especially in the absence of any judicial proceedings—would mean letting the guilty back into "their home." The assistant chairman of the North Ossetian State Committee on Nationalities, for example, reflected, "It [the conflict] was aggression with the goal of seizing territory....And perhaps people can understand that when someone goes to you with a gun in hand and tries to take something, how can one talk about living together?"[185] Third, the mechanism of return is deeply flawed. So-called "conciliatory commissions" actually act as a filtration system, arbitrarily denying return of Ingush based on dubious and tendentious evidence. Fourth, the June 1994 agreement on the return of the displaced stipulates that homes and infrastructure must be rebuilt before Ingush can return, but a less then reliable flow of funds from Moscow has made reconstruction difficult. Finally the general insecurity and continued presence of illegal armed groups in the regions hinders reconciliation and return. The last three obstacles will be addressed here.[186]

---

[184] "Ekho Moskvy," (Moscow), Foreign Broadcast Information Service (FBIS), Central Eurasia, August 21, 1995, p. 40.

[185] Human Rights Watch/Helsinki interview with Kabolov.

[186] For discussion of accountability, see section entitled, "Accountability and Justice in the Prigorodnyi Conflict."

Conclusion of the Conflict

On October 25, 1993, representatives from both Ingushetiya and North Ossetia signed an agreement creating the conciliatory commissions.[187] To facilitate reconciliation and the return of Ingush displaced, these groups, which consist of seven Ingush and Osssetian village representatives from the village in question, are supposed to approve those Ingush who wish to return to their homes in the Prigorodnyi region.[188]

In fact, however, the conciliatory commissions appear to be stacked in favor of Ossetians, hinder the return of displaced Ingush to their homes in the Prigorodnyi region, and hence do little to achieve conciliation between the two communities. While commission rulings are only supposed to be taken as recommendations, Ossetian members seem to excercise absolute veto power. For example, in July 1994 the Conciliatory Commission of the village of Chermen—without the participation of its Ingush members—rejected forty-five of fifty-three families who had applied to return to Chermen because "villagers suspected them of committing crimes."

More troublesome still, after an Ingush family is nominated for return, members of the commission seek out information—which does not seem to be verified by any independent body—to reject the candidate. In addition, Ossetian families do not seem to have to be vetted through the commission to return to the village. Finally, members of the commission are elected in open voting by the village as a whole, even though the majority of villagers are against the return of the Ingush.[189] This leads to the most radical villagers being chosen. One commission member from Chermen with whom Human Rights Watch spoke had lost her husband in the fighting. He was taken hostage and his mutilated body was found several months later. She told us that,

> If they come again, there will be more victims than in those days. That I guarantee you....I work in the conciliatory

---

[187] *Raion Chrezvychainogo Polozheniya*, p. 6.

[188] "Cherez Dva Goda," pp. 36-7. Unless otherwise cited, information on the "conciliatory commissions" comes from this report.

[189] An Ossetian from Chermen whose house was destroyed told us, "I'm against the Ingush returning. I haven't seen anything good from them....There will never be peace. They even have a saying, "You are not an Ingush unless you killed an Ossetian." They always lived better than the Ossetians." Human Rights Watch/Helsinki interview, Chermen, North Ossetia, August 14, 1995.

commission, people asked me, they gave us a list, the husband participated but not the wife or kids, for example. Why do we let the wife here? The husband will follow. That will not be, it won't be. Never. If he comes he'll leave in a box. We'll control [who comes.] What do you do in such a situation? Neighbor knows neighbor, who did what. We had everything: two cars, cattle—nothing is left. And now he is supposed to be my neighbor. Understand me properly. Someone rapes your wife, and now you're supposed to live next door to him?[190]

During our visit to Chermen, Human Rights Watch was given a four-page newspaper that listed six hundred Ingush who had allegedly taken part in violent actions during the events of October-November 1992. The document stated:

[This is a] list of individuals who took part in the Ingush aggression of October-November 1992 against the Republic of North Ossetia as witnessed by the population of the Prigorodnyi region. This is published to ease the work of the conciliatory commission and of other organs that are dealing with the problem of carrying out the decree of the president of the Russian Federation. The return of participants in aggression and their families to the villages of the Prigorodnyi region is equivalent to restarting the conflict in an even more violent form.

The list's accuracy is questionable. It is divided into sections, the first of which deals with instigators of the conflict; Russia's human rights commissioner Sergei Kovalyev's name is among them.

An Ingush family from Nazran reported that because they fled the village of Chermen and their home had been destroyed, the conciliatory commission there assumed they had taken part in the fighting and would not let them back in. The mother complained that,

The commission is operating there, they check something, they evaluate.....They write a list. So we applied [to return] in Nazran, and this list goes to the Temporary Administration, and they give

---

[190] Human Rights Watch/Helsinki interview, village of Chermen, North Ossetia, Russian Federation, August 14, 1994.

it to the Ossetians to be looked over. And what do they do, they cross out half, as if this half took part in military activities. If you don't have a home [because it was destroyed] they think that you fought and [so] left. We were pulled from the list completely.[191]

Another serious obstacle to the speedy return of Ingush displaced to Prigorodnyi is the overwhelming destruction in the region, especially of Ingush homes, the majority of which were wantonly destroyed after the conflict ended. North Ossetians, along with Russian authorities, insist that the damaged infrastructure be restored and homes rebuilt before anyone is allowed to return. The Ingush, on the other hand, want to return immediately and start repairing homes themselves. The sluggish disbursement of reconstruction funds by Moscow authorities slows the process of return.[192] According to Vladimir Lozovoi, only thirty-nine billion rubles of the five hundred billion needed for the restoration of the Prigorodnyi region was received from federal authorites in 1994-1995.[193] In September 1995, Valentin Burdin, acting head of the Temporary State Committee, complained that poor financing and slow constructive work was hampering Ingush return.[194] In February 1996, after it had been announced that the Russian government would appropriate six hundred billion rubles to reconstruction in

---

[191] Human Rights Watch/Helsinki interview, village of Maiskii, North Ossetia, Russian Federation, August 14, 1994.

[192] North Ossetian officials also expressed bewilderment at the fact that the needs of Ingush displaced seemed to take priority over those of the tens of thousands of Ossetian refugees from Georgia (including South Ossetia) living in North Ossetia. A North Ossetian official complained to Human Rights Watch that, "I have to say that on the territory of North Ossetia there is a huge number of refugees and displaced of all nationalities. But for some reason the main attention goes to the Ingush. Things connected with refugees have to be worked out in a 'complex solution,' A refugee, whether from South Ossetia, Georgia, or Prigorodnyi, is a refugee and has to be given the same treatment." Human Rights Watch/Helsinki interview with Kabolov.

[193] Natalya Gorodetskaya, "Prezidenty Severnoi Osetii I Ingushetiya otkazalis' ot territorial'nykh pretenzii" (The Presidents of North Ossetia and Ingushetiya Renounce Territorial Claims"), *Segodnya* (Moscow), July 12, 1995, p. 2.

[194] Moscow, ITAR-TASS, Foreign Broadcast Information Service (FBIS), Central Eurasia, September 11, 1995, p. 52.

Prigorodnyi, Temporary State Committee head Vladimir Lozovoi complained that, "in spite of the fact that it [600 billion rubles] should have been sent by the personal order of Boris Yeltsin, we—judging by everything—are not really expecting it."[195]

A Russian Foreign Ministry official involved in the Ossetian-Ingush negotiations rejected the Ingush demand that all displaced simply return to their homes and live in temporary shelters until they can rebuild their homes. He told Human Rights Watch that, "Above all, a return should be appropriate, safe, well-prepared and should be in accordance with the wishes of those who are returning. We believe that such a hasty manner, simply to pull up trailers and send off people, and to call this repatriation, is not right."[196] A North Ossetian official involved in the returning process echoed the Russian position but complains of the lack of funds from the center:

> Suppose there is a rational politician who does not seek conflict but seeks the resolution of conflict, how would he react if someone suggested to him to house on the territory of our republic refugees in trailers ["vagonchiki"], who have lived two years in the neighboring republic in very bad conditions. Also, taking into account that the official leadership, that is Russia, already passed several decrees about giving us tens of billions of rubles, eighty billion in total, but the money doesn't come. They don't give the money for the restoration of those homes on our territory that were blown up and burned, destroyed to their foundations. You have the absolute absence of living conditions for those who should return. So you settle this bitter people on an empty field, in trailers. But who will supply all these trailers. That is still not clear to us. There is no water because the water mains have been blown up, all lines of communication have been destroyed, and people will become even more embittered....We make one demand on our part: that the money that has been appropriated officially by Russia, by which the President issued an order and the government a decree signed by Chernomyrdin, must be given out. We will use this money to

---

[195] Gorodetskaya, February 7, 1996.

[196] Human Rights Watch/Helsinki interview with Lebedev, August 1994.

restore homes where possible, but above all to put in working order our gas and water lines and sewers.[197]

In a December 1995 interview, North Ossetian President Galazov repeated this philosophy, commenting that "We are being hurried [to return Ingush diplaced] and they don't consider that the return of Ingush refugees under pressure, on ground that is unprepared and can have the completely opposite result."[198]

The inability of the authorities to remove the large number of illegal weapons in circulation and the existence of paramilitary groups that engage in criminal and destabilizing activity also prevent normalization of the situation and the return of the displaced to the Prigorodnyi region.[199] Until the outbreak of hostilities in Chechnya in December 1994, weapons were sold freely there and continued to flow into Ingushetiya through a largely uncontrolled border. Paramilitary groups often act in conjunction with official security organs in both Ingushetiya and North Ossetia. In North Ossetia they operate in the guise of the Directorate for the Protection of Objects of the National Economy (UOONKH).

---

[197] Human Rights Watch/Helsinki interview with Tsoriyev.

[198] Petr Pliyev, "Prezident vidit svet v kontse tunnelya," (President sees light at the end of the tunnel"), *Nezavisimaya Gazeta* (Moscow), January 1, 1996, p. 3.

[199] See section, "The Arming of Ossetians and Ingush" on armed groups. For crimes committed by paramilitary groups, see section, "1992-1994: Violations of the Rules of War in the Ingush-Ossetian Conflict".

Almost no one in the region disputes the dangerously high quantity of weapons in society. One North Ossetian deputy told Human Rights Watch that, "There are lots of armed people. From this side and that side. And they are not controllable....There are 49,000 [Ossetian] refugees from Georgia who do not have residency permits. Some have refugee status, others have nothing. And I'm sure that each family has a Kalashnikov" Human Rights Watch/Helsinki interview with Lagkuyev, Ossetia, August 15, 1994.

The head of the administration in Chermen commented that, "They fire out of anything. We don't have ICBMs, but everything else we have. Automatics, grenade launchers, machine guns. These are the weapons that remained after the fighting ended. Also Chechens bring weapons in and sell them." Human Rights Watch/Helsinki interview, village of Chermen, North Ossetia, Russian Federation, August 15, 1994. Officials from the Temporary Administration made similar statements.

While paramilitary groups were disbanded in Ingushetiya in December 1992, none of their weapons were confiscated.[200]

The UOONKH was formed by a North Ossetian government decree in the spring of 1993 on the basis of popular militias already existing since the fighting in 1992.[201] According to data from the former Temporary Administration, the UOONKH possesses roughly eighty APCs, two howitzers, three Alazan rocket launchers, about 1,500 automatic rifles, as well as anti-tank grenade launchers and sniper rifles.[202] Its formal duties were to guard "objects of the national economy", and villagers in Chermen told us that UOONKH members guarded the village generally, especially people working in the fields. During their August mission, Human Rights Watch researchers met an armed UOONKH member on patrol in the village of Tarskoye. Although the UOONKH was supposed to have been disbanded on May 28, 1994, UOONKH members could reapply for employment within the North Ossetian Ministry of the Interior. Vladimir Lozovoi, head of the former Temporary Administration, explained to Human Rights Watch the reasoning behind the measure: "You have to work with people. In this organization *there are both people with a criminal background* and people who are normal and just need to earn a living. You can't throw them [the normal ones] to fate."[203]

Although the former Temporary Administration and Russian authorities pledged from the first days of the conflict to disarm illegal groups and confiscate weapons, little success has been achieved. In January 1993, the head of the former Temporary Administration, A. Kotenkov, issued a decree calling for the disbanding of all armed units of the North Ossetian ASSR and the turning over of their

---

[200] "Cherez Dva Goda," pp. 54-55. Reports from reliable sources indicate that illegal armed Ingush groups have bases in the mountainous Dzheirakh region in the southern part of the republic. There are also reports that members of the Ingush Ministry of the Interior collude with these groups.

[201] Ibid, pp. 52-4. One popular militia, the North Ossetian Republican Guard, was put under the jurisdiction of the North Ossetian Interior Ministry.

See "Ya prodal stenku i kupil avtomat," ("I sold my furniture and bought an automatic,") *Pravda* (Moscow), June 29, 1994, p. 3, concerning the formation of the UOONKH and about its leader, ex-wrestler, Bimbolat Dzutsev, "Comrade Bibo."

The UOONKH is suspected in the seizure of six Ingush hostages on May 19, 1994.

[202] "Cherez Dva Goda," pp. 52-54.

[203] Human Rights Watch/Helsinki interview with Lozovoi. Author's italics.

Conclusion of the Conflict

weapons and military equipment to the North Ossetian Ministry of the Interior.[204] Former Temporary Administration chief Lozovoi told Human Rights Watch in August 1994 that major strides were being made in disarmament and in disbanding the UOONKH, but admitted that the process was difficult because many of these groups are under the roof of official structures: "In Ossetia this is the UOOKNH. This is a very powerful military structure. As of July 1, 1994, it has officially ceased to exist, but the process is still going on." In October 1994, the Russian human rights group "Memorial" stated that little disarmament had been achieved, especially of the UOONKH and its members. This lack of progress figured predominantly in a December 2, 1994, letter sent by President Yeltsin to authorities in Ingushetiya and North Ossetia, which noted "the large numbers of weapons being held by the population, [and] the unceasing acts of terrorism and violence."[205]

---

[204] "Severnaya Osetiya: Kakiye perspektyvy u Opolcheniya" ("North Ossetia: What are the prospects for the militias"), *Severnyi Kavkaz* (Vladikavkaz), January 30, 1993, p. 1.

[205] Moscow ITAR-TASS, Foreign Broadcast Information Service (FBIS), Central Eurasia, December 5, 1994.

VIII. RECENT DEVELOPMENTS

Tensions remained high between Ingush and Ossetians in the Prigorodnyi region of North Ossetia in 1995, and the war in neighboring Chechnya also had a destabilizing effect. When war broke out in Chechnya in December 1994, isolated shootings erupted in Ingushetiya. The village of Arshty on the border with Chechnya was bombed in January, and in other areas Ingush tried to block columns of Russian soldiers entering Chechnya leading to casualties on both sides. In a February 1995 press release, the Temporary Administration warned that groups sympathizing with "armed formations" in Chechnya were destabilizing the republic, and that same month Ingush President Aushev instituted a curfew in villages along the border with Chechnya.[206] Furthermore, clashes in Chechnya sent nearly 153,000 displaced into Ingushetiya by mid-April, a figure which rose to 161,024 by August.[207] Fighting also intensified along the Chechen-Ingush border as Chechen rebels turned the Chechen hill town of Bamut into a stronghold. Some Russian forces stationed in the Prigorodnyi region were transferred to Chechnya, causing manpower shortages.[208] In a bizarre raid in October 1995, Russian forces attacked the Ingush civilian airport at Sleptsovskaya killing several civilians.[209] Most recently, in February 1996, Russian troops reportedly shot dead seven civilians in Arshty and surrounded several other Ingush villages on the border with Chechnya.[210] Russian forces charged that they had been attacked and killed Dudayev fighters.

---

[206] "Na Puti Soglasiyu," *Vestnik* (Vladikavkaz), February 10, 1995, p. 1; "Aushev vvel Komendantskii Chas," ("Aushev has instituted a curfew,") *Izvesitiya* (Moscow), February 21, 1995.

[207] "Zamankho," (Nazran, Ingushetiya), Foreign Broadcast Information Service (FBIS), Central Eurasia, September 13, 1995, p. 44.

[208] Pliyev, *Nezavisimaya Gazeta*, October 27, 1995, p.3.

[209] "Obstrelyan Aeroport v Ingushetii," ("The airport in Ingushetiya is fired on,") *Segodnya,* Moscow, October 10, 1995.

[210] "Russian Troops Reportedly Attack Villages on Chechen-Ingush Border," *The Washington Post*, February 25, 1996.

There was not much improvement within the Prigorodnyi region. In February, the upper house of the Russian parliament failed to ratify an extension of the state of emergency in the Prigorodnyi region, and it was abolished. The Temporary Administration, which had enforced the state of emergency, lost the emergency rule powers it had rarely used and became known as the Temporary State Committee. In March Ingush authorities demanded the abolition of the Temporary State Committees and the removal of its chair, Vladimir Lozovoi, and the introduction of direct federal rule in Prigorodnyi.[211] A statement issued at the time by the Temporary State Committee declared the situation in Prigorodnyi unstable and blamed both Ingush and Ossetian authorities for the situation.[212] The statement continued that, "in fact, Ingush [in Prigorodnyi] are limited in their constitutional rights from protection against criminal encroachment, freedom of movement, free choice of workplace and type of occupation, [and] medical services...."[213] It also blamed North Ossetian security forces for not protecting Ingush and for not punishing "individuals who display aggressive behavior [to them] and provoke mass unrest."[214]

By spring, clashes again broke out between Ossetians and Ingush returning to their homes in the Prigorodnyi region. In March, it was reported that a fifty-year old Ingush woman was shot dead in Chermen.[215] In late April, there were reports that between thirty and fifty Ingush were stoned by Ossetians as they tried to enter Kurtat and Dongaron, two villages where Ingush were supposed to be able to return under President Yeltsin's December 1993 decree.[216] On May 22,

---

[211] Natalya Gorodetskaya, "Ingushetiya potrebovala vvesti federal'noye pravleniye v Prigorodnom raione" ("Ingushetiya Demands the Introduction of Federal Rule in the Prigorodnyi Region"), *Segodnya* (Moscow), March 6, 1995.

[212] Ibid.

[213] Ibid.

[214] Ibid.

[215] "V Prigorodnyi Raoine Severnoi Osetii obostrilas' obstanovka," ("The situation has become tense in the Prigorodnyi Region of North Ossetia,") *Izvestiya* (Moscow), March 2, 1995.

[216] Moscow-INTERFAX, Foreign Broadcast Information Service (FBIS), Central Eurasia, April 28, 1995; Ruslan Maysigov, "Ingush President Asks Yeltsin to Safeguard Refugee Rights," Moscow ITAR-TASS, FBIS, Central Eurasia, May 4, 1995; Moscow-ITAR-TASS,

a drunk North Ossetian policeman wounded two Ingush in Chermen, which caused a crowd to turn on the police, threatening to lynch them and shoot up their patrol car.[217] On June 22, in the village of Kurtat, unidentified persons fired at a column of Ingush displaced returning to their homes escorted by Russian and North Ossetian MVD forces.[218] One Ingush was killed and five wounded; three Ossetians were wounded. Before the firing broke out, a group of Ossetian demonstrators met the column.

A July 1995 meeting between President Ruslan Aushev of Ingushetiya and Askharbek Galazov of North Ossetia led to the signing of a joint protocol of an agreement intended to ease tensions: "On Measures for Carrying Out the Presidential Decree on Overcoming the Ossetian-Ingush Conflict." The core of the agreement was reportedly a mutual renunciation of territorial claims. By August, however, both sides were deadlocked in negotiations over the return of Ingush to the Prigorodnyi region. Ingush authorities blamed the Ossetian leadership for the slow pace of return, while the Ingush were blamed for raising territorial questions against Ossetia.[219] A meeting held at the end of September ended in failure, as Ingush and Ossetian negotiators could not agree on the rate or scale of the Ingush return to the Prigorodnyi region.[220]

Russian authorities led a new initiative in October, and on October 11, 1995, President Yeltsin met with both the Ingush and Ossetian presidents and

---

FBIS, Central Eurasia, May 5, 1995.

[217] Natalya Gorodetskaya, "Vitse-Prezident Ingushetii prosit vvesti v Prigorodnyi Raion voiska MVV RF" ("The Vice-President of Ingushetiya asks to have MVD troops sent to the Prigorodnyi Region,") *Segodnya* (Moscow), May 27, 1995, p. 2.

[218] Natalya Gorodetskaya, "Ingush, North Ossetian Presidents to Meet In July," *Segodnya* (Moscow), Foreign Broadcast Information Service (FBIS), Central Eurasia, June 27, 1995.

[219] Feliks Babitsky, "After the Euphoria, Deadlock," *Rossiskiye Vesti,* Foreign Broadcast Information Service (FBIS), August 18, 1995; "Ekho Moskvy," August 18, 1995.

[220] Moscow INTERFAX, Foreign Broadcast Information Service (FBIS), Central Eurasia, September 29, 1995, p. 39.

promised 700 billion rubles in reconstruction funds.²²¹ In that same month, the Russian Duma organized a committee to oversee implementation of Yeltsin's decrees on "liquidating" the aftermath of the conflict—including the return of Ingush displaced.²²² In November, Nikolai Yegorov, Yeltsin's advisor on inter-ethnic affairs, toured the Prigorodnyi region to investigate the repatriation process.²²³ At the end of November 1995, it was reported that Ingushetiya and North Ossetia would sign a treaty for the full normalization of relations and speedy repatriation of Ingush displaced. President Yeltsin even ordered the formation of a special commission head by Nationalities Minister Vyacheslav Mikhailov to work out a draft of such a treaty.²²⁴ This announcement came on the heels of the signing of the agreement, "On Measures for Carrying Out the Presidential Decree on Overcoming the Ossetian-Ingush Conflict," by the Ingush President Aushev and the North Ossetian head Galazov.²²⁵ The component of this agreement was the renunciation of mutual territorial claims.

But serious problems still remained, and the question of land still arose. According to a November 1995 statement by Temporary State Committee Lozovoi, North Ossetian security forces were not able to provide security for returning Ingush refugees and the action of Ingush and Federal forces were also ineffective

---

²²¹ Vladimir Sorokin, "Dogovor Budet Podpisan," ("The Agreement Will be Signed,") Nezavisimaya Gazeta, Moscow, November 17, 1995; Moscow INTERFAX, Foreign Broadcast Information Service (FBIS), Central Eurasia, November 15, 1995, p. 25.

Additionally, it was announced that a special mobile Interior Ministry Unit would be dispatched to the area under the command of Major General Georgii Zhukov.

²²² Natal'ya Gorodestkaya, "Gosduma Zainteresovalas' sud'boi Ingushskikh bezhentsev," ("The Duma has Interested Itself with the Fate of the Ingush Refugees,") *Sevodnya* (Moscow), October 19, 1995, p. 2.

²²³ Moscow INTERFAX, Foreign Broadcast Information Service (FBIS), Central Eurasia, November 13, 1995, p. 45.

²²⁴Natal'ya Gorodestkaya, "Boris Yeltsin Velel Ingushetii I Severnoi Osetii sotrudnichat," ("Yeltsin Ordered Ingushetiya and North Ossetia to Cooperate,") *Segodnya* (Moscow), November 3, 1995.

²²⁵Natal'ya Gorodetskaya, "Prezidenty Severnoi Osetii I Ingushetii otkazalis' ot vzaimnykh territorial'nykh pretenzii" (The Presidents of North Ossetia and Ingushetiya have renounced mutual territorial claims,") *Segodnya* (Moscow), December 1, 1995, p.2.

at this task.[226] He also complained that ending emergency rule in the region had a deleterious influence on security. By late January 1996, it also became apparent that no friendship treaty between North Ossetia and Ingushetiya would be signed: Ingush objected to language about border changes while Ossetian complained about the return of refugees.[227] Reportedly, the Ingush objected to Article 3 of the draft treaty, which stated that borders "can only be changed through mutual agreement and in accordance with the Russian Constitution."[228] They argued that Article 3 must be omitted from the draft because the borders of Ingushetiya had never been determined in the first place.[229] In a February 1996 interview, Lozovoi complained that the situation in Prigorodnyi could become extremely tense if action were not taken to solve the displaced Ingush crisis.[230]

---

[226] Natal'ya Gorodetskaya, "Tret'ya Godovshchina Osetino-Ingushskogo Konflikta proshla mirno," ("The Third Anniversary of the Ossetian-Ingush Conflict Passed Peacefully,") *Segodnya* (Moscow), November 2, 1995.

[227] Natal'ya Gorodetskaya, "Severnaya Osetiya i Ingushetiya ne mogut dogovorit'sya ne tol'ko o politike," ("North Ossetia and Ingushetiya cannot agree not only about politics,") *Segodnya* (Moscow), January 23, 1996.

[228] "Razrabotan Proyekt o Druzhbe Osetin and Ingushei," ("A Draft has been worked out concerning Friendship between Ossetians and Ingush,") *Segodnya* (Moscow), December 2, 1995, p.2.

[229] Ibid.

[230] Gorodetskaya, February 11, 1996.

IX. VIOLATIONS OF INTERNATIONAL HUMANITARIAN AND HUMAN RIGHTS LAW

Parties to the Ingush-Ossetian conflict are bound by international humanitarian law as it applies to the Russian Federation. The Russian Federation and subordinate state authorities are further bound by the International Covenant on Civil and Political Rights to which Russia is a party. All parties to the conflict have committed abuses that constitute violations of both branches of international law; most such abuses are also punishable as offenses under Russian criminal law as well.

International humanitarian law distinguishes between international and non-international or internal armed conflicts. The nature of hostilities in the Prigorodnyi region is that of an internal armed conflict, governed by Common Article 3 of the 1949 Geneva Conventions, to which Russia is a party. Both North Ossetia and Ingushetiya are constituent members of the Russian Federation, not independent states. Combat has primarily involved Ingush paramilitaries and North Ossetian security forces and militias, although Russian forces have at times engaged Ingush paramilitaries as well.

Common Article 3 to the Geneva Conventions expressly binds all parties to the internal conflict, including insurgents, although they do not have the legal capacity to sign the Geneva Conventions.[231] The application of the laws of war does not imply any recognition of the independence or belligerent status of the Ingush forces. Because the insurgents are not recognized as privileged combatants in an international armed conflict, they may be tried and punished by the Russian government for common crimes; for the same reason they neither enjoy prisoner of war status under the Geneva Conventions if captured. Russia and its security forces may, however, agree to treat captives as prisoners of war, and the Ingush forces may do the same.

---

[231] As private individuals within the national territory of a State party, certain obligations are imposed on them. International Committee of the Red Cross, *Commentary on the Additional Protocols of 1977* (Geneva: International Committee of the Red Cross, 1987) at 1345.

PROHIBITION OF ATTACKS AGAINST CIVILIANS

Attacks against the civilian population are prohibited by the laws of war. United Nations General Assembly Resolution 2444, adopted by unanimous vote on December 19, 1969, expressly recognized the customary law principle of civilian immunity and its complementary principle requiring the warring parties to distinguish civilians from combatants at all times.[232] The preamble to this resolution clearly states that these fundamental humanitarian law principles apply "in all armed conflicts," meaning both international and internal armed conflicts. United Nations Resolution 2444 affirms, ". . . the following principles for observance by all government and other authorities responsible for action in armed conflicts:

> (a) That the right of the parties to a conflict to adopt means of injuring the enemy is not unlimited;
>
> (b) That it is prohibited to launch attacks against the civilian populations as such;
>
> (c) That distinction must be made at all times between persons taking part in the hostilities and members of the civilian population to the effect that the latter be spared as much as possible.

Protocol I to the Geneva Conventions, which applies to international armed conflicts provides authoritative guidance in interpreting the prohibition of attacks on civilians. Article 57 of Protocol I, discussing the conduct of military operations, provides that "constant care shall be taken to spare the civilian population, civilians and civilian objects," and continues, "those who plan or decide upon an attack shall...take all feasible precautions in the choice of means and methods of attack with a view to avoiding, and in any event to minimizing, incidental loss of civilian life."

In situations of internal armed conflict, generally speaking, a civilian is any one who is not a member of the armed forces or of an organized armed group

---

[232] *Respect for Human Rights in Armed Conflicts*, United Nations Resolution 2444, G.A. Res. 2444, 23 U.N. GAOR Supp. (No. 18) at 164, U.N. Doc. A/7433 (1968).

of a party to the conflict. Accordingly, "the civilian population comprises all persons who do not actively participate in the hostilities."[233]

PROHIBITION OF INDISCRIMINATE ATTACKS: THE RULE OF PROPORTIONALITY

The prohibition of indiscriminate or disproportionate attacks is intimately connected to the prohibition on attacks on civilians.

Indiscriminate attacks include those "which are not directed at a specific military objective".[234] Among those methods specifically considered as indiscriminate in Protocol I are "bombardment by any methods or means which treats as a single military objective a number of clearly separated and distinct military objectives located in a city, town, village" or other area with a concentration of civilians or civilian objects, and attacks which may be expected to cause civilian deaths, injuries, or destruction of civilian objects "which would be excessive in relation to the concrete and direct military advantage anticipated."[235] Indiscriminate artillery or mortar attacks would also constitute "bombardment by any methods or means."

OTHER PROHIBITED ACTS

Common Article 3 which governs the conduct of internal armed conflicts states:

(1) Persons taking no active part in the hostilities, including members of armed forces who had laid down their arms and those placed *hors de combat* by sickness, wounds, detention, or any other cause, shall in all circumstances be treated humanely,

---

[233] R. Goldman, "International Humanitarian Law and the Armed Conflicts in El Salvador and Nicaragua," *American University Journal of International Law & Policy* 2 (1987), p. 553.

[234] Protocol I, Art. 51(4)(a) and (b).

[235] Protocol I Art. 51(5).

without any adverse distinction founded on race, colour, religion or faith, sex, birth or wealth, or any other similar criteria.

The provision goes on to list specific acts which are prohibited "at any time and in any place whatsoever" with respect to persons who take no active part in hostilities.

Violence to Life and Person

"Violence to life and person, in particular murder of all kinds, mutilation, cruel treatment and torture" is the first set of acts explicitly condemned by Article 3. These acts constitute grave abuses of human rights and are also punishable under Russian criminal law.

Hostage-Taking

Common Article 3 to the Geneva Conventions unambiguously forbids hostage-taking. "Hostages" are defined by the International Committee of the Red Cross as follows:

> [H]ostages are persons who find themselves, willingly or unwillingly, in the power of the enemy and who answer with their freedom or their life for compliance with the orders of the latter and for upholding the security of its armed forces.[236]

Hostage-taking is also punishable as kidnaping under Russian criminal law.

Humiliating or Degrading Treatment

"Outrages upon personal dignity, in particular humiliating or degrading treatment" is specifically prohibited by Common Article 3.

Looting or Pillage

Protocol II to the Geneva Conventions provides authoritative guidance in interpreting the requirement of "humane" treatment in Common Article 3. In addition to the foregoing acts against civilians, it includes "pillage" as an act that shall be prohibited at any time and at any place whatsoever. The prohibition covers both organized pillage and pillage resulting from isolated acts of indiscipline.[237]

---

[236] *ICRC Commentary* at 874.

[237] ICRC, *Commentary on the Additional Protocols*, p. 1376.

Violations of International Humanitarian and Human Rights Law

Displacement of Civilians and Attacks on Civilian Objects

Under Protocol II, which provides authoritative guidance to understanding the injunction to "humane" treatment of civilians, displacement of civilians for reasons related to the conflict is forbidden, with certain limited exceptions.

There are only two exceptions to the prohibition on displacement of civilians for war-related reasons: their security or imperative military reasons. Article 17 of Protocol II states:

> The displacement of the civilian population shall not be ordered for reasons related to the conflict unless the security of the civilians involved or imperative military reasons so demand. Should such displacements have to be carried out, all possible measures shall be taken in order that the civilian population may be received under satisfactory conditions of shelter, hygiene, health, safety and nutrition.

Displacement of civilians merely to deny a social base to the enemy has nothing to do with the security of the civilians, nor is it justified by "imperative military reasons," which require "the most meticulous assessment of the circumstances" because such reasons are so capable of abuse.[238]

In the Ingush-Ossetian conflict, displacement of civilians has taken place through systematic destruction of houses and infrastructure belonging to the enemy ethnic group. Deliberate attacks on civilian houses, schools, churches, hospitals and other objects are also forbidden. Only attacks on legitimate military targets are permissible. Legitimate military targets are defined in Protocol I as those "which by their nature, location, purpose or use" contribute effectively to the enemy's military action and "whose total or partial destruction, capture or neutralization, in the circumstances ruling at the time, offers a definite military advantage."[239] Where there is doubt whether a target normally dedicated to civilian purposes is being used to contribute effectively to military action, it shall be presumed not to be so used.

---

[238] ICRC, *Commentary on the Additional Protocols*, p. 1472.

[239] Protocol I Art. 51(5).

VIOLATIONS OF INTERNATIONALLY-RECOGNIZED HUMAN RIGHTS

As a party to the International Covenant on Civil and Political Rights (ICCPR) Russia is bound to protect the rights therein, even in times of conflict. From November 2, 1992 to January 31, 1995, Russia declared a state of emergency in the Prigorodnyi region of North Ossetia, as well as in contiguous areas of North Ossetia and Ingushetiya, which it registered with the United Nations Treaty Office. Under the state of emergency, Russia exercised the option of derogating from certain rights under Article 4 of the ICCPR, in particular the rights of freedom of movement, freedom of expression, freedom of assembly, freedom of association.[240] However, the non-derogable rights to life and freedom from torture, or cruel, inhuman or degrading treatment or punishment continued to apply throughout the conflict, as did the right to liberty and security of person and freedom from arbitrary or unlawful interference with privacy, family and home.[241] Russia's obligation under the Covenant would not only be to refrain from violating these rights through its own agents, but to protect these rights from violation by others.

However, after they secured control of the Prigorodnyi region, Russian forces allowed North Ossetian Interior Ministry troops and North Ossetian paramilitaries—over whom they supposedly had control through a state of emergency decree—as well as South Ossetian militias, to conduct wide-scale looting and destruction of houses and communal dwellings. Russian forces have also been lax in punishing and bringing to justice Ingush and North Ossetian armed extremists who have preyed on the civilian population of the opposing ethnic group.

---

[240] ICCPR Articles 19(2) 21, 22(1), and 22(2) respectively. Article 4 permits derogation in extremely limited circumstances: "In time of public emergency which threatens the life of the nation and the existence of which is officially proclaimed," parties may derogate "to the extent strictly required by the exigencies of the situation, provided that such measures are not inconsistent with their other obligations under international law and do not involve discrimination on the ground of race, colour, sex, language, religion or social origin." Derogation under Article 4 would not in any way impair Russia's obligations under the laws of war.

[241] ICCPR Articles 6(1), 7 and 9(1), 17 respectively.